GOLF RULES ILLUSTRATED

EIGHTH EDITION

COMPILED BY
THE ROYAL AND ANCIENT GOLF CLUB OF ST ANDREWS

ILLUSTRATIONS BY
PETER DAVIDSON

FOREWORD

I have much pleasure in presenting the Eighth edition of
Golf Rules Illustrated.

This Edition incorporates the 1996 Rules of Golf as agreed
between the Royal & Ancient Golf Club of St. Andrews and the
United States Golf Association in consultation with golfing
bodies throughout the world. Once again, no major changes
have been introduced but a number of Rules have been amended
in continuance of the policy of making the Rules of Golf as
clear as possible.

With the ever increasing popularity of the game throughout the
world, golf is being played by a greater number of people and
interest in the Rules continues to grow. We hope that the many
illustrated examples of popular situations contained herein will
provide useful guidance to all players of the game, whether they
are just starting or have played for many years.

DAVID I. PEPPER, Chairman,
Rules of Golf Committee,
Royal & Ancient Golf Club of St. Andrews

Reprinted 1996
Printed in Spain by Graphy Cems, Morentin (Navarra)

This revised and updated edition published in 1996
by Hamlyn, an imprint of Reed Consumer Books Ltd
Michelin House, 81 Fulham Road, London SW3 6RB
and Auckland, Melbourne, Singapore and Toronto

Text copyright © 1996 Royal & Ancient Golf Club
Design copyright © 1996 Reed International Books Ltd

ISBN 0 600 58715 0

A CIP catalogue record for this book is available at the British Library

CONTENTS

SECTION 1
ETIQUETTE

COURTESY ON THE COURSE

Safety: Prior to playing a stroke or making a practice swing, the player should ensure that no one is standing close by or in a position to be hit by the club, the ball or any stones, pebbles, twigs or the like which may be moved by the stroke or swing.

Consideration for Other Players: The player who has the honour should be allowed to play before his opponent or fellow-competitor tees his ball.

No one should move, talk or stand close to or directly behind the ball or the hole when a player is addressing the ball or making a stroke.

No player should play until the players in front are out of range.

Pace of Play: In the interest of all, players should play without delay.

Players searching for a ball should signal the players behind them to pass as soon as it becomes apparent that the ball will not easily be found. They should not search for five minutes before doing so. They should not continue play until the players following them have passed and are out of range.

When the play of a hole has been completed, players should immediately leave the putting green.

If a match fails to keep its place on the course and loses more than one clear hole on the players in front, it should invite the match following to pass.

When taking a practice swing, a player should always make sure that no one is standing where they might be hit.

If a group is holding up the players behind and has lost more than a hole on the players in front, it should invite them to play through.

PRIORITY ON THE COURSE

In the absence of special rules, two-ball matches should have precedence over and be entitled to pass any three- or four-ball match, which should invite them through.

A single player has no standing and should give way to a match of any kind.

Any match playing a whole round is entitled to pass a match playing a shorter round.

CARE OF THE COURSE

Holes in Bunkers: Before leaving a bunker, a player should carefully fill up and smooth overall holes and footprints made by him.

Replace Divots: Repair Ball Marks and Damage by Spikes. Through the green, a player should ensure that any turf cut or displaced by him is replaced at once and pressed down and that any damage to the putting green made by a ball is carefully repaired. *On completion of the hole* by all players in the group, damage to the putting green caused by golf shoe spikes should be repaired.

Damage to Greens - Flagsticks, Bags, etc: Players should ensure that, when putting down bags or the flagstick, no damage is done to the putting green and that neither they nor their caddies damage the hole by standing close to it, in handling the flagstick or in removing the ball from the hole. The flagstick should be properly replaced in the hole before the players leave the putting green. Players should not damage the putting green by leaning on their putters, particularly when removing the ball from the hole.

Golf Carts: Local notices regulating the movement of golf carts should be strictly observed.

Damage through Practice Swings: In taking practice swings, players should avoid causing damage to the course, particularly the tees, by removing divots.

Always repair divots (bottom right), carefully repair pitch marks on the putting green (centre) and smooth over footprints and other marks when leaving a bunker (below). Do not lean on your putter when removing the ball from the hole (top).

SECTION 2
DEFINITIONS

The Definitions are placed in alphabetical order and some are also repeated at the beginning of their relevant Rule.
In the Rules themselves, defined terms which may be important to the application of a Rule are emphasised in bold the first time

ADDRESSING THE BALL

Except in a hazard, a player has addressed the ball when he has taken his stance and grounded his club.

In a bunker or water hazard a player has addressed the ball when he has taken his stance.

The player has decided not to ground his putter. Therefore, he has not "addressed the ball" and cannot be penalised under Rule 18-2b.

Addressing the Ball: A player has "addressed the ball" when he has taken his **stance** and has also grounded his club, except that in a **hazard** a player has addressed the ball when he has taken his stance.

Advice: "Advice" is any counsel or suggestion which could influence a player in determining his play, the choice of a club or the method of making a **stroke.**

Information on the Rules or on matters of public information, such as the position of hazards or the flagstick on the putting green, is not advice.

Ball Deemed to Move: See "Move or Moved"

Ball Holed: See "Holed"

Ball Lost: See "Lost Ball"

Ball in Play: A ball is "in play" as soon as the player has made a **stroke** on the **teeing ground**. It remains in play until holed out, except when it is **lost**, **out of bounds** or lifted, or another ball has been substituted whether or not such substitution is permitted; a ball so substituted becomes the ball in play.

Bunker: A "bunker" is a **hazard** consisting of a prepared area of ground, often a hollow, from which turf or soil has been removed and replaced with sand or the like. Grass-covered ground bordering or within a bunker is not part of the bunker. The margin of a bunker extends vertically downwards, but not upwards. A ball is in a bunker when it lies in or any part of it touches the bunker.

Caddie: A "caddie" is one who carries or handles a player's clubs during play and otherwise assists him in accordance with the Rules.

When one caddie is employed by more than one player, he is always deemed to be the caddie of the player whose ball is involved, and **equipment** carried by him is deemed to be that player's equipment, except when the caddie acts upon specific directions of another player, in which case he is considered to be that other player's caddie.

Casual Water: "Casual water" is any temporary accumulation of water on the **course** which is visible before or after the player takes his **stance** and is not in a **water hazard**. Snow and natural ice, other than frost, are either casual water or **loose impediments**, at the option of the player. Manufactured ice is an **obstruction**. Dew and frost are not casual water.

A ball is in casual water when it lies in or any part of it touches the casual water.

Committee: The "Committee" is the committee in charge of the competition or, if the matter does not arise in a competition, the committee in charge of the course.

Competitor: A "competitor" is a player in a stroke competition. A "fellow-competitor" is any person with whom the competitor plays. Neither is **partner** of the other.

In stroke play foursome and four-ball competitions, where the context so admits, the word "competitor" or "fellow-competitor" includes his partner.

Caddie
A caddie will carry a player's clubs and offer advice on club selection, the direction of play and line for putting.

7

Course: The "course" is the whole area within which play is permitted (see Rule 33-2).

Equipment: "Equipment" is anything used, worn or carried by or for the player except any ball he has played at the hole being played and any small object, such as a coin or a tee, when used to mark the position of a ball or the extent of an area in which a ball is to be dropped. Equipment includes a golf cart, whether or not motorised. If such a cart is shared by two or more players, the cart and everything in it are deemed to be the equipment of the player whose ball is involved except that, when the cart is being moved by one of the players sharing it, the cart and everything in it are deemed to be that player's equipment.

Note: A ball played at the hole being played is equipment when it has been lifted and not put back into play.

EQUIPMENT

Equipment includes a golf cart. As it is not being moved by one of the players, the cart and everything in it are deemed to be the equipment of the player whose ball is involved.

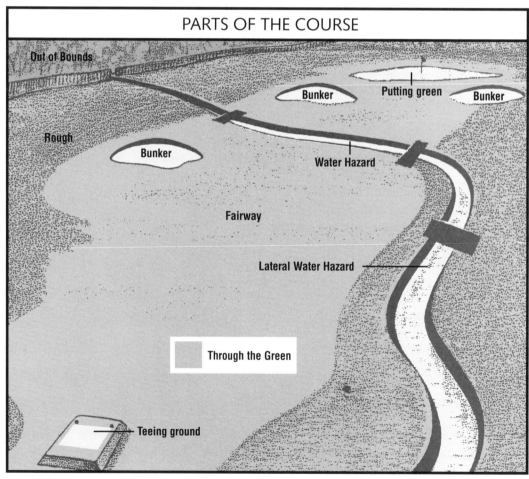

PARTS OF THE COURSE

Out of Bounds

Bunker

Putting green

Bunker

Rough

Bunker

Water Hazard

Fairway

Lateral Water Hazard

Through the Green

Teeing ground

GROUND UNDER REPAIR

Fellow-Competitor: See " Competitor"

Flagstick: The "flagstick" is a movable straight indicator, with or without bunting or other material attached, centred in the hole to show its position. It shall be circular in cross-section.

Forecaddie: A "forecaddie" is one who is employed by the Committee to indicate to players the position of balls during play. He is an **outside agency**.

Ground Under Repair: "Ground under repair" is any portion of the **course** so marked by order of the Committee or so declared by its authorised representative. It includes material piled for removal and a hole made by a greenkeeper, even if not so marked. Stakes and lines defining ground under repair are in such ground. Stakes defining ground under repair are obstructions. The margin of ground under repair extends vertically downwards, but not upwards. A ball is in ground under repair when it lies in or any part of it touches the ground under repair.

Note 1: Grass cuttings and other material left on the the course which have been abandoned and are not intended to be removed are not ground under repair unless so marked.

Note 2: The Committee may make a Local Rule prohibiting play from ground under repair or an environmentally-sensitive area which has been defined as ground under repair.

Hazards: A "hazard" is any **bunker** or **water hazard**.

Hole: The "hole" shall be 4 1⁄4 inches (108 mm) in diameter and at least 4 inches (100 mm) deep. If a lining is used, it shall be sunk at least 1 inch (25 mm) below the **putting green** surface unless the nature of the soil makes it impracticable to do so; its outer diameter shall not exceed 4 1⁄4 inches (108 mm).

Holed: A ball is "holed" when it is at rest within the circumference of the hole and all of it is below the level of the lip of the hole.

Honour: The side entitled to play first from the **teeing ground** is said to have the "honour".

Lateral Water Hazard: A "lateral water hazard" is a **water hazard** or that part of a water hazard so situated that it is not possible or is deemed by the Committee to be impracticable to drop a ball behind the water hazard in accordance with Rule 26-1b.

That part of a water hazard to be played as a lateral water hazard should be distinctively marked. A ball is in a lateral water hazard when it lies in or any part of it touches the lateral water hazard.

Note 1: Lateral water hazards should be defined by red stakes or lines.

Note 2: The Committee may make a Local Rule prohibiting play from an environmentally sensitive area which has been defined as a lateral water hazard.

Line of Play: The "line of play" is the direction which the player wishes his ball to take after a stroke, plus a reasonable distance on either side of the intended direction. The line of play extends vertically upwards from the ground, but does not extend beyond the hole.

Line of Putt: The "line of putt" is the line which the player wishes his ball to take after a stroke on the **putting green**. Except with respect to Rule 16-1e, the line of putt includes a reasonable distance on either side of the intended line. The line of putt does not extend beyond the hole.

Loose Impediments: "Loose impediments" are natural objects such as stones, leaves, twigs, branches and the like, dung, worms and insects and casts or heaps made by them, provided they are not fixed or growing, are not solidly embedded and do not adhere to the ball.

Sand and loose soil are loose impediments on the **putting green**, but not elsewhere.

Snow and natural ice, other than frost, are

LOOSE IMPEDIMENTS OR MOVABLE OBSTRUCTIONS

Natural objects such as:
branches, stones, dead rat, worm casts, fir cones, leaves, insects

Artificial/manufactured objects such as:
tin can, tee, booklet, rake, bottle, litter, score card

10

BALL DEEMED TO MOVE

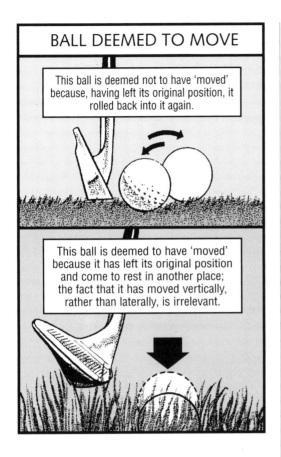

This ball is deemed not to have 'moved' because, having left its original position, it rolled back into it again.

This ball is deemed to have 'moved' because it has left its original position and come to rest in another place; the fact that it has moved vertically, rather than laterally, is irrelevant.

either **casual water** or loose impediments, at the option of the player. Manufactured ice is an **obstruction**.

Dew and frost are not loose impediments.

Lost Ball: A ball is "lost" if:
a. It is not found or identified as his by the player within five minutes after the player's side or his or their caddies have begun to search for it; or
b. The player has put another ball into play under the Rules, even though he may not have searched for the original ball; or
c. The player has played any stroke with a **provisional ball** from the place where the original ball is likely to be or from a point nearer the hole than that place, whereupon the provisional ball becomes the **ball in play**.

Time spent in playing a wrong ball is not counted in the five-minute period allowed for search.

Marker: A "marker" is one who is appointed by the Committee to record a competitor's score in stroke play. He may be a **fellow-competitor**. He is not a referee.

Matches: See "Sides and Matches".

Move or Moved: A ball is deemed to have "moved" if it leaves its position and comes to rest in any other place.

Observer: An "observer" is one who is appointed by the Committee to assist a **referee** to decide questions of fact and to report to him any breach of a Rule. An observer should not attend the flagstick, stand at or mark the position of the hole, or lift the ball or mark its position.

Obstructions: An "obstruction" is anything artificial, including the artificial surfaces and sides of roads and paths and manufactured ice, except:
a. Objects defining **out of bounds**, such as walls, fences, stakes and railings;
b. Any part of an immovable artificial object which is out of bounds; and

OBSTRUCTIONS

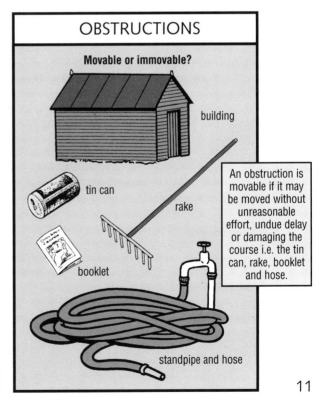

Movable or immovable?

building

tin can

rake

booklet

standpipe and hose

An obstruction is movable if it may be moved without unreasonable effort, undue delay or damaging the course i.e. the tin can, rake, booklet and hose.

c. Any construction declared by the Committee to be an integral part of the course.

Out of Bounds: "Out of bounds" is ground on which play is prohibited.

When out of bounds is defined by reference to stakes or a fence or as being beyond stakes or a fence, the out of bounds line is determined by the nearest inside points of the stakes or fence posts at ground level excluding angled supports.

When out of bounds is defined by a line on the ground, the line itself is out of bounds.

The out of bounds line extends vertically upwards and downwards.

A ball is out of bounds when all of it lies out of bounds.

A player may stand out of bounds to play a ball lying within bounds.

Outside Agency: An "outside agency" is any agency not part of the match or, in stroke play, not part of the competitor's side, and includes a referee, a marker, an observer and a forecaddie. Neither wind nor water is an outside agency.

Partner: A "partner" is a player associated with another player on the same side.

In a threesome, foursome, best-ball or four-ball match, where the context so admits, the word "player" includes his partner or partners.

Penalty Stroke: A "penalty stroke" is one added to the score of a player or **side** under certain Rules. In a threesome or foursome, penalty strokes do not affect the order of play.

Provisional Ball: A "provisional ball" is a ball played under Rule 27-2 for a ball which may be **lost** outside a water hazard or may be out of bounds.

Putting Green: The "putting green" is all ground of the hole being played which is specially prepared for putting or otherwise defined as such by the Committee. A ball is on the putting green when any part of it touches the putting green.

Referee: A "referee" is one who is appointed by the Committee to accompany players to decide questions of fact and apply the Rules. He shall act on any breach of a Rule which he observes or is reported to him.

A referee should not attend the flagstick, stand at or mark the position of the hole, or lift the ball or mark its position.

Rub of the Green: A "rub of the green" occurs when a ball in motion is accidentally deflected or stopped by any **outside agency** (see Rule 19-1).

Rule: The term "Rule" includes Local Rules made by the Committee under Rule 33-8a.

Sides and Matches:

Side: A player, or two or more players who are partners.

Single: A match in which one plays against another.

Threesome: A match in which one plays against two, and each side plays one ball.

Foursome: A match in which two play against two, and each side plays one ball.

Three-ball: A match play competition in which three play against one another, each playing his own ball. Each player is playing two distinct matches.

Best-ball: A match in which one plays against the better ball of two or the best ball of three players.

Four-ball: A match in which two play their better ball against the better ball of two other players.

Stance: Taking the "stance" consists in a player placing his feet in position for and preparatory to making a stroke.

Stipulated Round: The "stipulated round" consists of playing the holes of the course in their correct sequence unless otherwise authorised by the Committee. The number of holes in a stipulated round is 18 unless a smaller number is authorised by the

TEEING GROUND

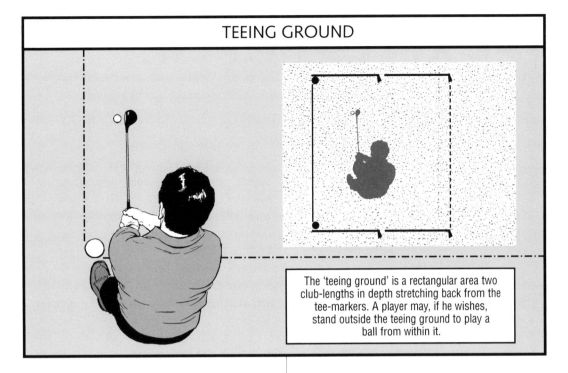

The 'teeing ground' is a rectangular area two club-lengths in depth stretching back from the tee-markers. A player may, if he wishes, stand outside the teeing ground to play a ball from within it.

Committee. As to extension of stipulated round in match play, see Rule 2-3.

Stroke: A "stroke" is the forward movement of the club made with the intention of fairly striking at and moving the ball, but if a player checks his downswing voluntarily before the clubhead reaches the ball he is deemed not to have made a stroke.

Teeing Ground: The "teeing ground" is the starting place for the hole to be played. It is a rectangular area two club-lengths in depth, the front and the sides of which are defined by the outside limits of two tee-markers. A ball is outside the teeing ground when all of it lies outside the teeing ground.

Through the Green: "Through the green" is the whole area of the **course** except:
a. The **teeing ground** and **putting green** of the hole being played; and
b. All **hazards** on the course.

Water Hazard: A "water hazard" is any sea, lake, pond, river, ditch, surface drainage ditch or other open water course (whether or not containing water) and anything of a similar nature.

All ground or water within the margin of a water hazard is part of the water hazard. The margin of a water hazard extends vertically upwards and downwards. Stakes and lines defining the margins of water hazards are in the hazards. Such stakes are obstructions. A ball is in a water hazard when it lies in or any part of it touches the water hazard.
Note 1: Water hazards (other than **lateral water hazards**) should be defined by yellow stakes or lines.
Note 2: The Committee may make a Local Rule prohibiting play from an environmentally-sensitive area which has been defined as a water hazard.

Wrong Ball: A "wrong ball" is any ball other than the player's:
a. **Ball in play**,
b. **Provisional ball** or
c. Second ball played under Rule 3-3 or Rule 20-7b in stroke play.
Note: Ball in play includes a ball substituted for the ball in play whether or not such substitution is permitted.

13

SECTION 3

THE RULES OF PLAY

1 | THE GAME

RULE 1-1
GENERAL

The Game of Golf consists in playing a ball from the **teeing ground** into the hole by a stroke or successive **strokes** in accordance with the Rules.

RULE 1-2
EXERTING INFLUENCE ON BALL

No player or caddie shall take any action to influence the position or the movement of a ball except in accordance with the Rules.

PENALTY FOR BREACH OF RULE 1-2: *Match Play — Loss of hole; Stroke play — Two strokes.*

Note: In the case of a serious breach of Rule 1-2, the Committee may impose a penalty of disqualification.

MATCH PLAY: AGREEMENT TO CONSIDER HOLE HALVED

An agreement to halve a hole being played does not of itself constitute an agreement to waive the Rules.

EQUITY- SOME EXAMPLES

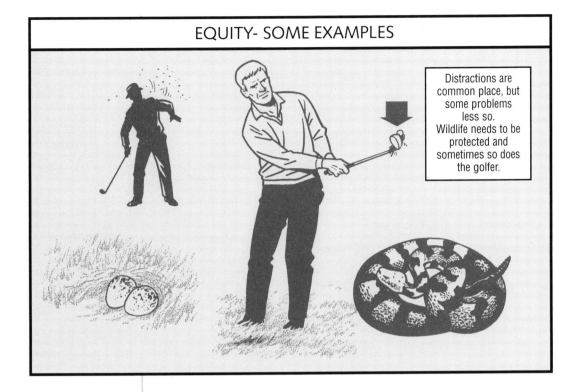

Distractions are common place, but some problems less so. Wildlife needs to be protected and sometimes so does the golfer.

RULE 1-3
AGREEMENT TO WAIVE RULES

Players shall not agree to exclude the operation of any Rule or to waive any penalty incurred.

PENALTY FOR BREACH OF RULE 1-3: *Match play — Disqualification of both sides; Stroke play — Disqualification of competitors concerned.*

(Agreeing to play out of turn in stroke play — see Rule 10-2c.)

RULE 1-4
POINTS NOT COVERED BY RULES

If any point in dispute is not covered by the Rules, the decision shall be made in accordance with equity.

2 MATCH PLAY

RULE 2-1
WINNER OF HOLE; RECKONING OF HOLES

In match play the game is played by holes.

Except as otherwise provided in the Rules, a hole is won by the side which holes its ball in the fewer strokes. In a handicap match the lower net score wins the hole.

The reckoning of holes is kept by the terms: so many "holes up" or "all square", and so many "to play".

A side is "dormie" when it is as many holes up as there are holes remaining to be played.

RULE 2-2
HALVED HOLE

A hole is halved if each side holes out in the same number of strokes.

When a player has holed out and his opponent has been left with a stroke for the half, if the player thereafter incurs a penalty, the hole is halved.

RULE 2-3
WINNER OF MATCH

A match (which consists of a **stipulated round**, unless otherwise decreed by the Committee) is won by the side which is leading by a number of holes greater than the number of holes remaining to be played.

The Committee may, for the purpose of settling a tie, extend the stipulated round to as many holes as are required for a match to be won.

RULE 2-4
CONCESSION OF NEXT STROKE, HOLE OR MATCH

When the opponent's ball is at rest or is deemed to be at rest under Rule 16-2, the player may concede the opponent to have holed out with his next stroke and the ball may be removed by either side with a club or otherwise.

A player may concede a hole or a match at any time prior to the conclusion of the hole or the match.

Concession of a stroke, hole or match may not be declined or withdrawn.

RULE 2-5
CLAIMS

In match play, if a doubt or dispute arises between the players and no duly authorised representative of the Committee is available within a reasonable time, the players shall continue the match without delay. Any claim, if it is to be considered by the Committee, must be made before any player in the match plays from the next teeing ground or, in the case of the last hole of the match, before all players in the match leave the putting green.

No later claim shall be considered unless it is based on facts previously unknown to the player making the claim and the player making the claim had been given wrong information (Rules 6-2a and 9) by an opponent. In any case, no later claim shall be considered after the result of the match has been officially announced, unless the Committee is satisfied that the opponent knew he was giving wrong information.

RULE 2-6
GENERAL PENALTY

The penalty for a breach of a Rule in match play is loss of hole except when otherwise provided.

3 STROKE PLAY

RULE 3-1
WINNER

The competitor who plays the **stipulated round** or rounds in the fewest strokes is the winner.

DOUBT AS TO PROCEDURE IN STROKE PLAY

> I'm not sure whether I can get free relief from this path. I'll play out the hole with two balls, this ball as it lies and then another ball having taken a drop away from the path. I would like the second ball to count.

> That's fine, I'll record both scores and we'll get a decision from the Committee when we get in.

RULE 3-2
FAILURE TO HOLE OUT

a *Procedure*

If a competitor fails to hole out at any hole and does not correct his mistake before he plays a **stroke** from the next **teeing ground** or, in the case of the last hole of the round, before he leaves the **putting green**, *he shall be disqualified.*

RULE 3-3
DOUBT AS TO PROCEDURE

In stroke play only, when during play of a hole a competitor is doubtful of his rights or procedure, he may, without penalty, play a second ball. After the situation which caused the doubt has arisen, the competitor should, before taking further action, announce to his marker or a fellow-competitor his decision to invoke this Rule and the ball with which he will score if the Rules permit.

The competitor shall report the facts to the **Committee** before returning his score card unless he scores the same with both balls; if he fails to do so, *he shall be disqualified.*

b *Determination of Score for Hole*

If the Rules allow the procedure selected in advance by the competitor, the score with the ball selected shall be his score for the hole.

If the competitor fails to announce in advance his decision to invoke this Rule or his selection, the score with the original ball or, if the original ball is not one of the balls being played, the first ball put into play shall count if the Rules allow the procedure adopted for such ball.

Note: A second ball played under Rule 3-3 is not a provisional ball under Rule 27-2.

RULE 3-4
REFUSAL TO COMPLY WITH A RULE

If a competitor refuses to comply with a Rule affecting the rights of another competitor, *he shall be disqualified.*

RULE 3-5
GENERAL PENALTY

The penalty for a breach of a Rule in stroke play is two strokes except when otherwise provided.

CLUBS AND THE BALL

The Royal and Ancient Golf Club of St. Andrews and the United States Golf Association reserve the right to change the Rules and make and change the interpretations relating to clubs, balls and other implements at any time.

CLUBS

A player in doubt as to the conformity of a club should consult the Royal and Ancient Golf Club of St. Andrews.

A manufacturer may submit to the Royal and Ancient Golf Club of St. Andrews a sample of a club which is to be manufactured for a ruling as to whether the club conforms with Rule 4 and Appendix II. Such sample will become the property of the Royal and Ancient Golf Club of St. Andrews for reference purposes. If a manufacturer fails to submit a sample before manufacturing and/or marketing the club, he assumes the risk of a ruling that the club does not conform with the Rules of Golf.

Where a club, or part of a club, is required to have some specific property, this means that it must be designed and manufactured with the intention of having that property. The finished club or part must have that property within manufacturing tolerances appropriate to the material used.

RULE 4-1
FORM AND MAKE OF CLUBS

A club is an implement designed to be used for striking the ball. A putter is a club with a loft not exceeding ten degrees designed primarily for use on the putting green. The player's clubs shall conform with the provisions of this Rule and with the specifications and interpretations set forth in Appendix II

a *General*

The club shall be composed of a shaft and a head. All parts of the club shall be fixed so that the club is one unit. The club shall not be designed to be adjustable except for weight (see also Appendix II). The club shall not be substantially different from the traditional and customary form and make, and shall have no external attachments except as otherwise permitted by the Rules.

b *Shaft*

The shaft shall be straight, with the same bending and twisting properties in any direction, and shall be attached to the clubhead at the heel either directly or through a single plain neck and/or socket. A putter shaft may be attached to any point in the head.

c *Grip*

The grip consists of that part of the shaft designed to be held by the player and any material added to it for the purpose of obtaining a firm hold. The grip shall be straight and plain in form, shall extend to the end of the shaft and shall not be moulded for any part of the hands.

d *Clubhead*

The distance from the heel to the toe of the clubhead shall be greater than the distance from the face to the back. The clubhead shall be generally plain in shape. The clubhead shall have only one striking face, except that a putter may have two such faces if their characteristics are the same, and they are opposite each other.

e *Club Face*

The face of the club shall be hard and rigid (some exceptions may be made for putters) and, except for such markings as are permitted by Appendix II, shall be smooth and shall not have any degree of concavity.

f *Wear and Alteration*

A club which conforms with Rule 4-1 when new is deemed to conform after wear through normal use. Any part of a club which has been

CLUB BROKEN IN NORMAL COURSE OF PLAY

I've broken my club playing that shot. Can I replace it?

Yes, but in doing so you may not unduly delay play or borrow a club being used by anyone playing on the course.

purposely altered is regarded as new and must conform, in the altered state, with the Rules.

g *Damage*

If a player's club ceases to conform with Rule 4-1 because of damage sustained in the normal course of play, the player may:
(i)   use the club in its damaged state, but only for the remainder of the **stipulated round** during which such damage was sustained; or
(ii) without unduly delaying play, repair it.
A club which ceases to conform because of damage sustained other than in the normal course of play shall not subsequently be used during the round.
(Damage changing playing characteristics of club — see Rule 4-2.)
(Damage rendering club unfit for play — see Rule 4-4a.)

RULE 4-2
PLAYING CHARACTERISTICS CHANGED
During a **stipulated round**, the playing characteristics of a club shall not be purposely changed by adjustment or by any other means.

If the playing characteristics of a player's club are changed during a round because of damage sustained in the normal course of play, the player may:
(i)   use the club in its altered state; or
(ii) without unduly delaying play, repair it.
If the playing characteristics of a player's club are changed because of damage sustained other than in the normal course of play, the club shall not subsequently be used during the round.
Damage to a club which occurred prior to a round may be repaired during the round, provided the playing characteristics are not changed and play is not unduly delayed.

RULE 4-3
FOREIGN MATERIAL
Foreign material must not be applied to the club face for the purpose of influencing the movement of the ball.
PENALTY FOR BREACH OF RULE 4-1, -2 or -3: *Disqualification.*

RULE 4-4
MAXIMUM OF FOURTEEN CLUBS

a *Selection and Replacement of Clubs*

The player shall start a **stipulated round** with not more than fourteen clubs. He is limited to the clubs thus selected for that round except that, without unduly delaying play, he may:
(i)   if he started with fewer than fourteen clubs, add any number provided his total number does not exceed fourteen; and
(ii) replace, with any club, a club which becomes unfit for play in the normal course of play.
The addition or replacement of a club or clubs may not be made by borrowing any club selected for play by any other person playing on the course.

b *Partners May Share Clubs*

Partners may share clubs, provided that the total number of clubs carried by the partners so sharing does not exceed fourteen.

PENALTY FOR BREACH OF RULE 4-4a or b, REGARDLESS OF NUMBER OF EXCESS CLUBS CARRIED: *Match play — At the conclusion of the hole at which the breach is discovered, the state of the match shall be adjusted by deducting one hole for each hole at which a breach occurred. Maximum deduction per round: two holes.*
Stroke play — Two strokes for each hole at which any breach occurred; maximum penalty per round: four strokes.
Bogey and par competitions — Penalties as in match play.
Stableford competitions — see Note to Rule 32-1b.

c *Excess Club Declared Out of Play*

Any club carried or used in breach of this Rule shall be declared out of play by the player immediately upon discovery that a breach has occurred and thereafter shall not be used by the player during the round.

PENALTY FOR BREACH OF RULE 4-4c: *Disqualification.*

5 THE BALL

RULE 5-1
GENERAL

The ball the player uses shall conform to requirements specified in Appendix III on maximum weight, minimum size, spherical symmetry, initial velocity and overall distance.

Note: The Committee may require, in the conditions of a competition (Rule 33-1), that the ball the player uses must be named on the current List of Conforming Golf Balls issued by the Royal and Ancient Golf Club of St. Andrews.

RULE 5-2
FOREIGN MATERIAL

Foreign material must not be applied to a ball for the purpose of changing its playing characteristics.

PENALTY FOR BREACH OF RULE 5-1 or 5-2: *Disqualification.*

RULE 5-3
BALL UNFIT FOR PLAY

A ball is unfit for play if it is visibly cut, cracked or out of shape. A ball is not unfit for play solely because mud or other materials adhere to it, its surface is scratched or scraped or its paint is damaged or discoloured.

If a player has reason to believe his ball has become unfit for play during the play of the hole being played, he may during the play of such hole lift his ball without penalty to determine whether it is unfit.

Before lifting the ball, the player must announce his intention to his opponent in match play or his marker or a fellow-competitor in stroke play and mark the position of the ball. He may then lift and examine the ball without cleaning it and must give his opponent, marker or fellow-competitor an opportunity to examine the ball.

If he fails to comply with this procedure, *he shall incur a penalty of one stroke*.

If it is determined that the ball has become unfit for play during play of the hole being played, the player may substitute another ball, placing it on

BALL UNFIT FOR PLAY

the spot where the original ball lay. Otherwise, the original ball shall be replaced.

If a ball breaks into pieces as a result of a stroke, the stroke shall be cancelled and the player shall play a ball without penalty as nearly as possible at the spot from which the original ball was played (see Rule 20-5).

PENALTY FOR BREACH OF RULE 5-3: *Match play — Loss of hole; Stroke play — Two strokes.*

If a player incurs the general penalty for breach of Rule 5-3, no additional penalty under the Rule shall be applied.

Note: If the opponent, marker or fellow-competitor wishes to dispute a claim of unfitness, he must do so before the player plays another ball. (Cleaning ball lifted from putting green or under any other Rule — see Rule 21.)

6 THE PLAYER

DEFINITION

A "marker" is one who is appointed by the Committee to record a **competitor's** *score in stroke play. He may be a* **fellow-competitor**. *He is not a* **referee**.

RULE 6-1
CONDITIONS OF COMPETITION

The player is responsible for knowing the conditions under which the competition is to be played (Rule 33-1).

RULE 6-2
HANDICAP

Before starting a match in a handicap competition, the players should

a *Match Play*

determine from one another their respective handicaps. If a player begins the match having declared a higher handicap which would affect the number of strokes given or received, *he shall be disqualified*; otherwise, the player shall play off the declared handicap.

b *Stroke Play*

In any round of a handicap competition, the competitor shall ensure that his handicap is recorded on his score card before it is returned to the Committee. If no handicap is recorded on his score card before it is returned, or if the recorded handicap is higher than that to which he is entitled and this affects the number of strokes received, *he shall be disqualified* from that round of the handicap competition; otherwise, the score shall stand. *Note*: It is the player's responsibility to know the holes at which handicap strokes are to be given or received.

RULE 6-3
TIME OF STARTING AND GROUPS

a *Time of Starting*

The player shall start at the time laid down by the Committee.

b *Groups*

In stroke play, the competitor shall remain throughout the round in the group arranged by the Committee unless the Committee authorises or ratifies a change.

PENALTY FOR BREACH OF RULE 6-3: *Disqualification.*

(Best-ball and four-ball play — see Rules 30-3a and 31-2.)

Note: The Committee may provide in the conditions of a competition (Rule 33-1) that, if the player arrives at his starting point, ready to play, within five minutes after his starting time, in the absence of circumstances which warrant waiving the penalty of disqualification as provided in Rule 33-7, the penalty for failure to start on time is *loss of the first hole in match play or two strokes at the first hole in stroke play* instead of disqualification.

RULE 6-4
CADDIE

The player may have only one **caddie** at any one time, *under penalty of disqualification*.

For any breach of a Rule by his caddie, the player incurs the applicable penalty.

RULE 6-5
BALL

The responsibility for playing the proper ball rests with the player. Each player should put an identification mark on his ball.

RULE 6-6
SCORING IN STROKE PLAY

a *Recording Scores*

After each hole the **marker** should check the score with the competitor and record it. On completion of the round the marker shall sign the card and hand it to the competitor. If more than one marker records the scores, each shall sign for the part for which he is responsible.

25

PLAYER'S RESPONSIBILITIES

SCORING IN STROKE PLAY

COMPETITION __SPRING STROKE PLAY__   DATE __14 . 6 . 95__

PLAYER __D. BROWN__   HANDICAP __10__   Game No __21__

Hole	Yards	Par	Stroke Index	Score	W+L-H=0 POINTS	Mar Score	Hole	Yards	Par	Stroke Index	Score	W+L-H=0 POINTS	Mar Score
1	312	4	17	5		6	10	369	4	12	̶6̶ 5 c		
2	446	4	1	4		4	11	433	4	2	3		
3	310	4	13	4		3	12	361	4	14	4		
4	370	4	9	5	b	5	13	415	4	6	5		
5	478	5	3	6			14	155	3	16	6		
̶8̶7	429	4	11	4			15	338	4	8	5		
̶7̶6	385	4	5	3			16	316	4	10	4		
8	178	3	7	4			17	191	3	4	5		
9	354	4	15	6			18	508	5	18	7		
OUT	3262			41			IN	3086	35		44		
							OUT	3262	36		41		
							TOTAL	6348	71		85		

Markers Signature __D.B.__ e & f

HANDICAP __10__ d
NETT __75__

Players Signature __Bill White__

Competitor's Responsibilities:
1 To record the correct handicap somewhere on the score card before it is returned to the Committee.
2 To check the gross score recorded for each hole is correct.
3 To ensure that the marker has signed the card and to countersign the card himself before it is returned to the Committee.

Committee Responsibilities:
1 Issue to each competitor a score card containing the date and the competitor's name.
2 To add the scores for each hole and apply the handicap recorded on the card.

(**a**) Hole numbers may be altered if hole scores have been recorded in the wrong boxes.
(**b**) A marker need not keep a record of his own score, however it is recommended.
(**c**) There is nothing in the Rules that requires an alteration to be initialled.
(**d**) The competitor is responsible only for the correctness of the score recorded for each hole. If the competitor records a wrong total score or net score, the Committee must correct the error, without penalty to the competitor. In this instance, the Committee have added the scores for each hole and applied the handicap.
(**e**) There is no penalty if a marker signs the competitor's score card in the space provided for the competitor's signature, and the competitor then signs in the space provided for the marker's signature.
(**f**) The initialing of the score card by the competitor is sufficient for the purpose of countersignature.

26

b *Signing and Returning Card*

After completion of the round, the competitor should check his score for each hole and settle any doubtful points with the Committee. He shall ensure that the marker has signed the card, countersign the card himself and return it to the Committee as soon as possible.

PENALTY FOR BREACH OF RULE 6-6B: *Disqualification.*

c *Alteration of Card*

No alteration may be made on a card after the competitor has returned it to the Committee.

d *Wrong Score for Hole*

The competitor is responsible for the correctness of the score recorded for each hole on his card. If he returns a score for any hole lower than actually taken, *he shall be disqualified*. If he returns a score for any hole higher than actually taken, the score as returned shall stand.

Note 1: The Committee is responsible for the addition of scores and application of the handicap recorded on the card — see Rule 33-5.

Note 2: In four-ball stroke play, see also Rule 31-4 and -7a.

RULE 6-7
UNDUE DELAY; SLOW PLAY

The player shall play without undue delay and in accordance with any pace of play guidelines which may be laid down by the Committee. Between completion of a hole and playing from the next teeing ground, the player shall not unduly delay play.

PENALTY FOR BREACH OF RULE 6-7: *Match play — Loss of hole; Stroke play — Two Strokes.*

For subsequent offence — Disqualification.

Note 1: If the player unduly delays play between holes, he is delaying the play of the next hole and the penalty applies to that hole.

UNDUE DELAY: ENTERING CLUBHOUSE

PACE OF PLAY

In order to help prevent slow play, the Committee may lay down pace of play guidelines and penalise any player or players who play too slowly.

Note 2: For the purpose of preventing slow play, the Committee may, in the conditions of a competition (Rule 33–1), lay down pace of play guidelines including maximum periods of time allowed to complete a stipulated round, a hole or a stroke.

In stroke play only, the Committee may, in such a condition modify the penalty for a breach of this Rule as follows:

First offence – One stroke; Second offence – Two strokes. For subsequent offence – Disqualification.

RULE 6-8
DISCONTINUANCE OF PLAY

a *When Permitted* The player shall not discontinue play unless:

(i) the Committee has suspended play;

(ii) he believes there is danger from lightning;

(iii) he is seeking a decision from the Committee on a doubtful or disputed point (see Rules 2-5 and 34-3); or

(iv) there is some other good reason such as sudden illness.

Bad weather is not of itself a good reason for discontinuing play.

If the player discontinues play without specific permission from the Committee, he shall report to the Committee as soon as practicable. If he does so and the Committee considers his reason satisfactory, the player incurs no penalty. Otherwise, *the player shall be disqualified.*

Exception in match play: Players discontinuing match play by agreement are not subject to disqualification unless by so doing the competition is delayed.

Note: Leaving the course does not of itself constitute discontinuance of play.

b *Procedure When Play Suspended by Committee*

When play is suspended by the Committee, if the players in a match or group are between the play of two holes, they shall not resume play until the Committee has ordered a resumption of play. If they are in the process of playing a hole, they may continue provided they do so without delay. If they choose to continue, they shall discontinue either before or immediately after completing the hole, and shall not thereafter resume play until the Committee has ordered a resumption of play.

When play has been suspended by the Committee, the player shall resume play when the Committee has ordered a resumption of play.

PENALTY FOR BREACH OF RULE 6-8B: *Disqualification.* PENALTY

Note: The Committee may provide in the conditions of a competition (Rule 33–1) that, in potentially dangerous situations, play shall be discontinued immediately following a suspension of play by the Committee. If a player fails to discontinue play immediately, *he shall be disqualified* unless circumstances warrant waiving such penalty as provided in Rule 33–7. (Resumption of play – see Rule 33–2d.)

c *Lifting Ball When Play Discontinued*

When during the play of a hole a player discontinues play under Rule 6-8a, he may lift his ball. A ball may be cleaned when so lifted. If a ball has been so lifted, the player shall, when play is resumed, place a ball on the spot from which the original ball was lifted.

PENALTY FOR BREACH OF RULE 6-8C: *Match play — Loss of hole; Stroke play — Two strokes.*

Practice putting and chipping on or near the tee of the next hole to be played is permitted as long as play is not delayed.

 # PRACTICE

RULE 7-1
BEFORE OR BETWEEN ROUNDS

a *Match Play*

On any day of a match play competition, a player may practise on the competition **course** before a round.

b *Stroke Play*

On any day of a stroke competition or play-off, a competitor shall not practise on the competition **course** or test the surface of any putting green on the course before a round or play-off. When two or more rounds of a stroke competition are to be played over consecutive days, practice between those rounds on any competition course remaining to be played is prohibited.

Exception: Practice putting or chipping on or near the first **teeing ground** before starting a round or play-off is permitted.

PENALTY FOR BREACH OF RULE 7-1b: *Disqualification.*

Note: The Committee may in the conditions of a competition (Rule 33-1) prohibit practice on the competition course on any day of a match play competition or permit practice on the competition course or part of the course (Rule 33-2c) on any day of or between rounds of a stroke competition.

RULE 7-2
DURING ROUND

A player shall not play a practice **stroke** either during the play of a hole or between the play of two holes except that, between the play of two holes, the player may practise putting or chipping on or near the **putting green** of the hole last played, any practice putting green or the **teeing ground** of the next hole to be played in the round, provided such practice stroke is not played from a hazard and does not unduly delay play (Rule 6-7).

Strokes played in continuing the play of a hole, the result of which has been decided, are not practice strokes.

Exception: When play has been suspended by the Committee, a player may, prior to resumption of play, practise (a) as provided in this Rule, (b) anywhere other than on the competition course and (c) as otherwise permitted by the Committee.

PENALTY FOR BREACH OF RULE 7-2: *Match play — Loss of hole: Stroke play — Two strokes.*

In the event of a breach between the play of two holes, the penalty applies to the next hole.

*Note 1: A practice swing is not a practice **stroke** and may be taken at any place, provided the player does not breach the Rules.*

*Note 2: The Committee may prohibit practice on or near the **putting green** of the hole last played.*

8 ADVICE; INDICATING LINE OF PLAY

DEFINITIONS

*"Advice" is any counsel or suggestion which could influence a player in determining his play, the choice of a club or the method of making a **stroke**.*

Information on the Rules or on matters of public information, such as the position of hazards or the flagstick on the putting green, is not advice.

The "line of play" is the direction which the player wishes his ball to take after a stroke, plus a reasonable distance on either side of the intended direction. The line of play extends vertically upwards from the ground, but does not extend beyond the hole.

RULE 8-1
ADVICE

During a **stipulated round,** a player shall not give **advice** to anyone in the competition except his partner. A player may ask for advice during a stipulated round from only his partner or either of their caddies.

RULE 8-2
INDICATING LINE OF PLAY

a *Other Than on Putting Green*

Except on the **putting green,** a player may have the **line of play** indicated to him by anyone, but no one shall be positioned by the player on or close to the line or an extension of the line beyond the hole while the **stroke** is being played. Any mark placed during the play of a hole by the player or with his knowledge to indicate the line shall be removed before the stroke is played. *Exception:* Flagstick attended or held up — see Rule 17-1.

b *On the Putting Green*

When the player's ball is on the **putting green,** the player, his partner or either of their caddies may, before but not during the **stroke,** point out a line for putting, but in so doing the putting green shall not be touched. No mark shall be placed anywhere to indicate a line for putting.

PENALTY FOR BREACH OF RULE: *Match play — Loss of hole: Stroke play — Two strokes.*

Note: The Committee may, in the conditions of a team competition (Rule 33–1), permit each team to appoint one person who may give **advice** (including pointing out a line for putting) to members of that team. The

Committee may lay down conditions relating to the appointment and permitted conduct of such person, who must be identified to the Committee before giving advice.

9 INFORMATION AS TO STROKES TAKEN

RULE 9-1
GENERAL

The number of strokes a player has taken shall include any penalty strokes incurred.

RULE 9-2
MATCH PLAY

A player who has incurred a penalty shall inform his opponent as soon as practicable, unless he is obviously proceeding under a Rule involving a penalty and this has been observed by his opponent. If he fails so to inform his opponent, he shall be deemed to have given wrong information, even if he was not aware that he had incurred a penalty.

An opponent is entitled to ascertain from the player, during the play of a hole, the number of strokes he has taken and, after play of a hole, the number of strokes taken on the hole just completed.

If during the play of a hole the player gives or is deemed to give wrong information as to the number of strokes taken, he shall incur no penalty if he

INFORMATION AS TO STROKES TAKEN

corrects the mistake before his opponent has played his next stroke. If the player fails so to correct the wrong information, *he shall lose the hole.*

If after play of a hole the player gives or is deemed to give wrong information as to the number of strokes taken on the hole just completed and this affects the opponent's understanding of the result of the hole, he shall incur no penalty if he corrects his mistake before any player plays from the next **teeing ground** or, in the case of the last hole of the match, before all players leave the **putting green**. If the player fails so to correct the wrong information, he shall lose the hole.

RULE 9-3
STROKE PLAY

A competitor who has incurred a penalty should inform his marker as soon as practicable.

10 ORDER OF PLAY

RULE 10-1
MATCH PLAY

a *Teeing Ground*

The side entitled to play first from the **teeing ground** is said to have the "honour".

The side which shall have the honour at the first teeing ground shall be determined by the order of the draw. In the absence of a draw, the honour should be decided by lot

The side which wins a hole shall take the honour at the next teeing ground. If a hole has been halved, the side which had the honour at the previous teeing ground shall retain it.

b *Other Than on Teeing Ground*

When the balls are in play, the ball farther from the hole shall be played first. If the balls are equidistant from the hole, the ball to be played first should be decided by lot.
Exception: Rule 30-3c (best-ball and four-ball match play).

c *Playing Out of Turn*

If a player plays when his opponent should have played, the opponent may immediately require the player to cancel the stroke so played and, in correct order, play a ball without penalty as nearly as possible at the spot from which the original ball was last played (see Rule 20-5).

RULE 10-2
STROKE PLAY

a *Teeing Ground*

The competitor entitled to play first from the **teeing ground** is said to have the "honour".

The competitor who shall have the honour at the first teeing ground shall be determined by the order of the draw. In the absence of a draw, the honour should be decided by lot.

The competitor with the lowest score at a hole shall take the honour at the next teeing ground.

The competitor with the second lowest score shall play next and so on. If two or more competitors have the same score at a hole, they shall play from the next teeing ground in the same order as at the previous teeing ground.

b *Other Than on Teeing Ground*

When the balls are in play, the ball farthest from the hole shall be played first. If two or more balls are equidistant from the hole, the ball to be played first should be decided by lot.
Exceptions: Rules 22 (ball interfering with or assisting play) and 31-5 (four-ball stroke play).

c *Playing Out of Turn*

If a competitor plays out of turn, no penalty is incurred and the ball shall be played as it lies. If, however, the Committee determines that competitors have agreed to play in an order other than that set forth in Clauses 2a and 2b of this Rule to give one of them an advantage, *they shall be disqualified.* (Incorrect order of play in threesomes and foursomes stroke play— see Rule 29-3.)

RULE 10-3
PROVISIONAL BALL OR SECOND BALL FROM TEEING GROUND

If a player plays a **provisional ball** or a second ball from a **teeing ground**, he should do so after his opponent or fellow-competitor has played his first **stroke**. If a player plays a provisional ball or a second ball out of turn, Clauses 1c and 2c of this Rule shall apply.

RULE 10-4
BALL MOVED IN MEASURING

If a ball is moved in measuring to determine which ball is farther from the hole, no penalty is incurred and the ball shall be replaced.

11 TEEING GROUND

DEFINITION

The "teeing ground" is the starting place for the hole to be played. It is a rectangular area two club-lengths in depth, the front and the sides of which are defined by the outside limits of two tee-markers. A ball is outside the teeing ground when all of it lies outside the teeing ground.

RULE 11-1
TEEING

In teeing, the ball may be placed on the ground, on an irregularity of surface created by the player on the ground, or on a tee, sand or other substance in order to raise it off the ground.

A player may stand outside the **teeing ground** to play a ball within it.

RULE 11-2
TEE-MARKERS

Before a player plays his first stroke with any ball from the teeing ground of the hole being played, the tee-markers are deemed to be fixed. In such

PLAYING FROM WRONG TEE IN STROKE PLAY

circumstances, if the player moves or allows to be moved a tee-marker for the purpose of avoiding interference with his stance, the area of his intended swing or his line of play, *he shall incur the penalty for a breach of Rule 13-2.*

RULE 11-3
BALL FALLING OFF TEE

If a ball, when not **in play**, falls off a tee or is knocked off a tee by the player in addressing it, it may be re-teed without penalty, but if a stroke is made at the ball in these circumstances, whether the ball is moving or not, the stroke counts but no penalty is incurred.

RULE 11-4
PLAYING FROM OUTSIDE TEEING GROUND

a *Match Play*

If a player, when starting a hole, plays a ball from outside the **teeing ground**, the opponent may immediately require the player to cancel the stroke so played and play a ball from within the teeing ground, without penalty.

b *Stroke Play*

If a competitor, when starting a hole, plays a ball from outside the **teeing ground**, *he shall incur a penalty of two strokes* and shall then play a ball from within the teeing ground.

If the competitor plays a stroke from the next teeing ground without first correcting his mistake or, in the case of the last hole of the round, leaves the **putting green** without first declaring his intention to correct his mistake, *he shall be disqualified.*

Strokes played by a competitor from outside the teeing ground do not count in his score.

RULE 11-5
PLAYING FROM WRONG TEEING GROUND
The provisions of Rule 11-4 apply.

12

SEARCHING FOR AND IDENTIFYING BALL

DEFINITIONS

A *"hazard" is any* **bunker** *or* **water hazard.**

A *"bunker" is a* **hazard** *consisting of a prepared area of ground, often a hollow, from which turf or soil has been removed and replaced with sand or the like. Grass-covered ground bordering or within a bunker is not part of the bunker. The margin of a bunker extends vertically downwards, but not upwards. A ball is in a bunker when it lies in or any part of it touches the bunker.*

A *"water hazard" is any sea, lake, pond, river, ditch, surface drainage ditch or other open water course (whether or not containing water) and anything of a similar nature.*

All ground or water within the margin of a water hazard is part of the water hazard. The margin of a water hazard extends vertically upwards and downwards. Stakes and lines defining the margins of water hazards are in the hazards. Such stakes are obstructions. A ball is in a water hazard when it lies in or any part of it touches the water hazard.

RULE 12-1
SEARCHING FOR BALL; SEEING BALL
In searching for his ball anywhere on the course, the player may touch or bend long grass, rushes, bushes, whins, heather or the like, but only to the extent necessary to find and identify it, provided that this does not improve

SEARCHING FOR BALL IN BUNKER

If a player's ball is buried in a bunker, he may search for it by probing the sand with his fingers or he may use a rake. If the ball is moved, there is no penalty, but it must be replaced and, if necessary, re-covered so that only part of it is visible.

the lie of the ball, the area of his intended swing or his line of play.

A player is not necessarily entitled to see his ball when playing a stroke.

In a **hazard**, if a ball is covered by **loose impediments** or sand, the player may remove by probing, raking or other means as much thereof as will enable him to see a part of the ball. If an excess is removed, no penalty is incurred and the ball shall be re-covered so that only a part of the ball is visible. If the ball is moved in such removal, no penalty is incurred; the ball shall be replaced and, if necessary, re-covered. As to removal of loose impediments outside a hazard, see Rule 23.

If a ball lying in **casual water, ground under repair** or a hole, cast or runway made by a burrowing animal, a reptile or a bird is accidentally moved during search, no penalty is incurred; the ball shall be replaced, unless the player elects to proceed under Rule 25-1b.

If a ball is believed to be lying in water in a **water hazard**, the player may probe for it with a club or otherwise. If the ball is moved in so doing, no penalty is incurred; the ball shall be replaced, unless the player elects to proceed under Rule 26-1.

PENALTY FOR BREACH OF RULE 12-1: *Match play — Loss of hole; Stroke play — Two strokes.*

RULE 12-2
IDENTIFYING BALL

The responsibility for playing the proper ball rests with the player. Each player should put an identification mark on his ball.

Except in a **hazard**, the player may, without penalty, lift a ball he believes to be his own for the purpose of identification and clean it to the extent necessary for identification. If the ball is the player's ball, he shall replace it. Before lifting the ball, the player must announce his intention to his opponent in match play or his marker or a fellow-competitor in stroke play and mark the position of the ball. He must then give his opponent, marker or fellow-competitor an opportunity to observe the lifting and replacement.

If he lifts his ball without announcing his intention in advance, marking the position of the ball or giving his opponent, marker or fellow-competitor an opportunity to observe, or if he lifts his ball for identification in a hazard, or cleans it more than necessary for identification, *he shall incur a penalty of one stroke* and the ball shall be replaced.

If a player who is required to replace a ball fails to do so, *he shall incur the penalty* for a breach of Rule 20-3a, but no additional penalty under Rule 12-2 shall be applied.

BALL PLAYED AS IT LIES; LIE, AREA OF INTENDED SWING AND LINE OF PLAY; STANCE

DEFINITIONS

A *"hazard"* is any **bunker** or **water hazard**.

A *"bunker"* is a **hazard** consisting of a prepared area of ground, often a hollow, from which turf or soil has been removed and replaced with sand or the like. Grass-covered ground bordering or within a bunker is not part of the bunker. The margin of a bunker extends vertically downwards, but not upwards. A ball is in a bunker when it lies in or any part of it touches the bunker.

A *"water hazard"* is any sea, lake, pond, river, ditch, surface drainage ditch or other open water course (whether or not containing water) and anything of a similar nature.

All ground or water within the margin of a water hazard is part of the water hazard. The margin of a water hazard extends vertically upwards and downwards. Stakes and lines defining the margins of water hazards are in the hazards. Such stakes are obstructions. A ball is in a water hazard when it lies in or any part of it touches the water hazard.

The *"line of play"* is the direction which the player wishes his ball to take after a stroke, plus a reasonable distance on either side of the intended direction. The line of play extends vertically upwards from the ground, but does not extend beyond the hole.

RULE 13-1
BALL PLAYED AS IT LIES
The ball shall be played as it lies, except as otherwise provided in the Rules. (Ball at rest moved — see Rule 18).

RULE 13-2
IMPROVING LIE, AREA OF INTENDED SWING OR LINE OF PLAY
Except as provided in the Rules, a player shall not improve or allow to be improved:

the position or lie of his ball,

the area of his intended swing,

his **line of play** or a reasonable extension of that line beyond the hole or

the area in which he is to drop or place a ball

by any of the following actions:

39

IMPROVING AREA OF INTENDED SWING OR LINE OF PLAY

A player must not break an interfering branch or remove sand which is off the putting green.

moving, bending or breaking anything growing or fixed (including immovable **obstructions** and objects defining **out of bounds**) or removing or pressing down sand, loose soil, replaced divots, other cut turf placed in position or other irregularities of surface

except as follows:

as may occur in fairly taking his **stance**,

in making a **stroke** or the backward movement of his club for a stroke,

on the **teeing ground** in creating or eliminating irregularities of surface, or

on the **putting green** in removing sand and loose soil as provided in Rule 16-1a or in repairing damage as provided in Rule 16-1c.

The club may be grounded only lightly and shall not be pressed on the ground.

Exception: Ball in hazard — see Rule 13-4.

RULE 13-3
BUILDING STANCE

A player is entitled to place his feet firmly in taking his stance, but he shall not build a stance.

RULE 13-4
BALL IN HAZARD

Except as provided in the Rules, before making a **stroke** at a ball which is in a **hazard** (whether a **bunker** or a **water hazard**) or which, having been lifted from a hazard, may be dropped or placed in the hazard, the player shall not:

a. Test the condition of the hazard or any similar hazard,

b. Touch the ground in the hazard or water in the water hazard with a club

BALL IN BUNKER

Before making a stroke at a ball which is in a bunker the player shall not:

... touch the ground with his club

... touch a loose impediment with his club at address or on his backswing

... remove loose impediments

... or smooth sand

or otherwise, or

c. Touch or move a **loose impediment** lying in or touching the hazard.

Exceptions:

1. Provided nothing is done which constitutes testing the condition of the hazard or improves the lie of the ball, there is no penalty if the player (a) touches the ground in any hazard or water in a water hazard as a result of or to prevent falling, in removing an **obstruction**, in measuring or in retrieving or lifting a ball under any Rule or (b) places his clubs in a hazard.

2. The player after playing the stroke, or his **caddie** at any time without the authority of the player, may smooth sand or soil in the hazard, provided that, if the ball is still in the hazard, nothing is done which improves the lie of the ball or assists the player in his subsequent play of the hole.

Note: At any time, including at address or in the backward movement for the stroke, the player may touch with a club or otherwise any obstruction, any construction declared by the Committee to be an integral part of the course or any grass, bush, tree or other growing thing.

PENALTY FOR BREACH OF RULE: *Match play — Loss of hole; Stroke play — Two strokes.*

(Searching for ball — see Rule 12-1.)

14 STRIKING THE BALL

DEFINITION

A "stroke" is the forward movement of the club made with the intention of fairly striking at and moving the ball, but if a player checks his downswing voluntarily before the clubhead reaches the ball he is deemed not to have made a stroke.

BALL TO BE FAIRLY STRUCK AT WITH CLUBHEAD

A player may strike the ball with the back or toe of the clubhead.

RULE 14-1
BALL TO BE FAIRLY STRUCK AT
The ball shall be fairly struck at with the head of the club and must not be pushed, scraped or spooned.

RULE 14-2
ASSISTANCE
In making a **stroke**, a player shall not accept physical assistance or protection from the elements.

PENALTY FOR BREACH OF RULE 14-1 or -2: *Match play — Loss of hole; Stroke play — Two strokes.*

RULE 14-3
ARTIFICIAL DEVICES AND UNUSUAL EQUIPMENT
A player in doubt as to whether use of an item would constitute a breach of Rule 14-3 should consult the Royal and Ancient Golf Club of St. Andrews.

A manufacturer may submit to the Royal and Ancient Golf Club of St. Andrews a sample of an item which is to be manufactured for a ruling as to whether its use during a stipulated round would cause a player to be in breach of Rule 14-3. Such sample will become the property of the Royal and Ancient Golf Club of St. Andrews for reference purposes. If a manufacturer fails to submit a sample before manufacturing and/or marketing the item, he assumes the risk of a ruling that use of the item would be contrary to the Rules of Golf.

Except as provided in the Rules, during a **stipulated round** the player shall not use any artificial device or unusual equipment

a. Which might assist him in making a stroke or in his play; or

b. For the purpose of gauging or measuring distance or conditions which might affect his play; or

c. Which might assist him in gripping the club, except that:

(i)   plain gloves may be worn;

(ii)   resin, powder and drying or moisturising agents may be used;

(iii)   tape or gauze may be applied to the grip (provided such application does not render the grip non-conforming under Rule 4-1c); and

(iv)   a towel or handkerchief may be wrapped around the grip.

PENALTY FOR BREACH OF RULE 14-3: *Disqualification.*

RULE 14-4
STRIKING THE BALL MORE THAN ONCE
If a player's club strikes the ball more than once in the course of a stroke, the player shall count the stroke and *add a penalty stroke,* making two strokes in all.

RULE 14-5
PLAYING MOVING BALL
A player shall not play while his ball is moving.

Exceptions:

Ball falling off tee — Rule 11-3.

43

PLAYING A SUBSTITUTED BALL

PLAYING WRONG BALL IN STROKE PLAY

Striking the ball more than once — Rule 14-4.

Ball moving in water — Rule 14-6.

When the ball begins to move only after the player has begun the **stroke** or the backward movement of his club for the stroke, he shall incur no penalty under this Rule for playing a moving ball, but he is not exempt from any penalty incurred under the following Rules:

Ball at rest moved by player — Rule 18-2a.

Ball at rest moving after loose impediment touched — Rule 18-2c.(Ball purposely deflected or stopped by player, partner or caddie – see Rule 1–2)

RULE 14-6
BALL MOVING IN WATER

When a ball is moving in water in a **water hazard,** the player may, without penalty, make a **stroke**, but he must not delay making his stroke in order to allow the wind or current to improve the position of the ball. A ball moving in water in a water hazard may be lifted if the player elects to invoke Rule 26.

PENALTY FOR BREACH OF RULE 14-5 or -6: *Match play — Loss of hole; Stroke play — Two strokes.*

15 WRONG BALL; SUBSTITUTED BALL

DEFINITION

A "wrong ball" is any ball other than the player's:
a. **Ball in play**,
b. **Provisional ball**, *or*
c. *Second ball played under Rule 3-3 or Rule 20-7b in stroke play.*
Note: Ball in play includes a ball substituted for the ball in play whether or not such substitution is permitted.

RULE 15-1
GENERAL

A player must hole out with the ball played from the **teeing ground** unless a Rule permits him to substitute another ball. If a player substitutes another ball when not so permitted, that ball is not a **wrong ball**; it becomes the **ball in play** and, if the error is not corrected as provided in Rule 20-6, *the player shall incur a penalty of loss of hole in match play or two strokes in stroke play.*(Playing from wrong place – see Rule 20–7).

RULE 15-2
MATCH PLAY

If a player plays a stroke with a **wrong ball** except in a **hazard**, *he shall lose the hole.*

If a player plays any strokes in a hazard with a wrong ball, there is no penalty. Strokes played in a hazard with a wrong ball do not count in the player's score. If the wrong ball belongs to another player, its owner shall place a ball on the spot from which the wrong ball was first played.

If the player and opponent exchange balls during the play of a hole, the first to play the wrong ball other than from a hazard shall lose the hole;

when this cannot be determined, the hole shall be played out with the balls exchanged.

RULE 15-3
STROKE PLAY

If a competitor plays a stroke or strokes with a **wrong ball**, *he shall incur a penalty of two strokes,* unless the only stroke or strokes played with such ball were played when it was in a hazard, in which case no penalty is incurred.

The competitor must correct his mistake by playing the correct ball. If he fails to correct his mistake before he plays a stroke from the next **teeing ground** or, in the case of the last hole of the round, fails to declare his intention to correct his mistake before leaving the **putting green**, *he shall be disqualified.*

Strokes played by a competitor with a wrong ball do not count in his score.

If the wrong ball belongs to another competitor, its owner shall place a ball on the spot from which the wrong ball was first played. (Lie of ball to be placed or replaced altered — see Rule 20-3b.)

16 THE PUTTING GREEN

The "putting green" is all ground of the hole being played which is specially prepared for putting or otherwise defined as such by the Committee. A ball is on the putting green when any part of it touches the putting green.

The "line of putt" is the line which the player wishes his ball to take after a stroke on the **putting green***. Except with respect to Rule 16-1e, the line of putt includes a reasonable distance on either side of the intended line. The line of putt does not extend beyond the hole.*

A ball is "holed" when it is at rest within the circumference of the hole and all of it is below the level of the lip of the hole.

RULE 16-1
GENERAL

a *Touching Line of Putt*

The **line of putt** must not be touched except:
(i) the player may move sand and loose soil on the putting green and other **loose impediments** by picking them up or by brushing them aside with his hand or a club without pressing anything down;
(ii) in addressing the ball, the player may place the club in front of the ball with-out pressing anything down;
(iii) in measuring — Rule 10-4;
(iv) in lifting the ball — Rule l6-lb;
(v) in pressing down a ball-marker;
(vi) in repairing old hole plugs or ball marks on the putting green — Rule l6-lc; and
(vii) in removing movable **obstructions** — Rule 24-1.
(Indicating line for putting on putting green — see Rule 8-2b.)

TOUCHING LINE OF PUTT: EXAMPLES OF WHEN PERMITTED

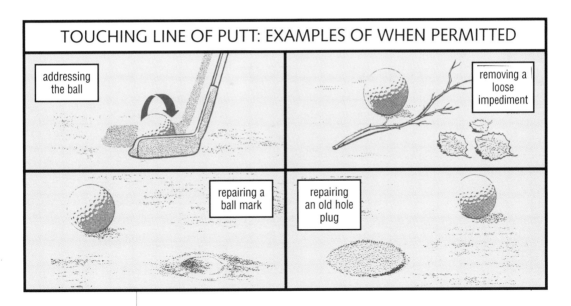

addressing the ball

removing a loose impediment

repairing a ball mark

repairing an old hole plug

b *Lifting Ball*

A ball on the **putting green** may be lifted and, if desired, cleaned. A ball so lifted shall be replaced on the spot from which it was lifted.

c *Repair of Hole, Plugs, Ball Marks and Other Damage*

The player may repair an old hole plug or damage to the putting green caused by the impact of a ball, whether or not the player's ball lies on the putting green. If the ball is moved in the process of such repair, it shall be replaced, without penalty. Any other damage to the putting green shall not

PROCEDURE FOR MARKING THE BALL

Do I have to use a ball-marker to mark my ball?

No. Although you are recommended to use a ball-marker or small coin, you may use something else like a tee peg or the putter head.

47

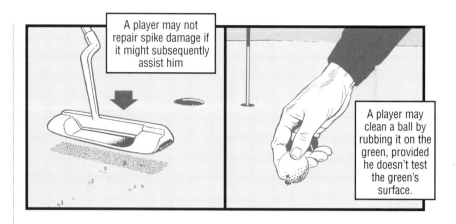

A player may not repair spike damage if it might subsequently assist him

A player may clean a ball by rubbing it on the green, provided he doesn't test the green's surface.

be repaired if it might assist the player in his subsequent play of the hole.

d *Testing Surface*

During the play of a hole, a player shall not test the surface of the **putting green** by rolling a ball or roughening or scraping the surface.

e *Standing Astride or On Line of Putt*

The player shall not make a **stroke** on the **putting green** from a **stance** astride, or with either foot touching, the line of putt or an extension of that line behind the ball.

f *Position of Caddie or Partner*

While making a stroke on the putting green, the player shall not allow his caddie, his partner or his partner's caddie to position himself on or close to an extension of the line of putt behind the ball.

g *Playing Stroke While Another Ball in Motion*

The player shall not play a stroke while another ball is in motion after a stroke from the putting green, except that, if a player does so, he incurs no

BALL OVERHANGING HOLE

How long may I wait to see if my ball will fall into the hole?

There's no point in waiting more than ten seconds. After that time the ball is deemed to be at rest and if it then falls in you have holed out with your last stroke, but you add a penalty stroke.

penalty if it was his turn to play.

(Lifting ball interfering with or assisting play while another ball in motion — see Rule 22.)

PENALTY FOR BREACH OF RULE 16-1: *Match play — Loss of hole; Stroke play — Two strokes.*

RULE 16-2
BALL OVERHANGING HOLE

When any part of the ball overhangs the lip of the hole, the player is allowed enough time to reach the hole without unreasonable delay and an additional ten seconds to determine whether the ball is at rest. If by then the ball has not fallen into the hole, it is deemed to be at rest. If the ball subsequently falls into the hole, the player is deemed to have holed out with his last stroke, and *he shall add a penalty stroke to his score* for the hole; otherwise there is no penalty under this Rule. (Undue delay — see Rule 6-7.).

17 THE FLAGSTICK

RULE 17-1
FLAGSTICK ATTENDED, REMOVED OR HELD UP

Before and during the stroke, the player may have the flagstick attended, removed or held up to indicate the position of the hole. This may be done

only on the authority of the player before he plays his stroke.

If, prior to the stroke, the flagstick is attended, removed or held up by anyone with the player's knowledge and no objection is made, the player shall be deemed to have authorised it. If anyone attends or holds up the flagstick or stands near the hole while a stroke is being played, he shall be deemed to be attending the flagstick until the ball comes to rest.

RULE 17-2
UNAUTHORISED ATTENDANCE

a *Match Play*

In match play, an opponent or his caddie shall not, without the authority or prior knowledge of the player, attend, remove or hold up the flagstick while the player is making a stroke or his ball is in motion.

b *Stroke Play*

In stroke play, if a fellow-competitor or his caddie attends, removes or holds up the flagstick without the competitor's authority or prior knowledge while the competitor is making a stroke or his ball is in motion, *the fellow-competitor shall incur the penalty* for breach of this Rule. In such circumstances, if the competitor's ball strikes the flagstick, the person attending it or anything carried by him, the competitor incurs no penalty and the ball shall be played as it lies, except that, if the stroke was played from the putting green, the stroke shall be cancelled, the ball replaced and the stroke replayed.

PENALTY FOR BREACH OF RULE 17-1 or -2: *Match play – Loss of hole; Stroke play – Two Strokes.*

RULE 17-3
BALL STRIKING FLAGSTICK OR ATTENDANT

The player's ball shall not strike:

a. The flagstick when attended, removed or held up by the player, his partner or either of their caddies, or by another person with the player's authority or prior knowledge; or

b. The player's caddie, his partner or his partner's caddie when attending the flagstick, or another person attending the flagstick with the player's authority or prior knowledge, or anything carried by any such person; or

c. The flagstick in the hole, unattended, when the ball has been played from the **putting green**.

PENALTY FOR BREACH OF RULE 17-3: *Match play – Loss of hole; Stroke play – Two strokes, and the ball shall be played as it lies.*

RULE 17-4
BALL RESTING AGAINST FLAGSTICK

If the ball rests against the flagstick when it is in the hole, the player or another person authorised by him may move or remove the flagstick and if the ball falls into the hole, the player shall be deemed to have holed out with his last stroke; otherwise the ball, if **moved,** shall be placed on the lip of the hole, without penalty.

18 BALL AT REST MOVED

DEFINITIONS

A ball is deemed to have "moved" if it leaves its position and comes to rest in any other place.

An "outside agency" is any agency not part of the match or, in stroke play, not part of the competitor's side, and includes a referee, a marker, an observer and a forecaddie. Neither wind nor water is an outside agency.

"Equipment" is anything used, worn or carried by or for the player

51

BALL AT REST MOVED

By Outside Agency - no penalty and replace ball (Rule 18-1)

By Player, Partner, Caddie or Equipment - one stroke penalty and replace ball (Rule 18-2a)

After Address - one stroke penalty and replace ball (Rule 18-2b)

After Loose Impediment Touched - if loose impediment within one club-length of ball, one stroke penalty and replace ball (Rule 18-2c)

By Opponent, Caddie or Equipment During Search - no penalty and replace ball (Rule 18-3a)

By Opponent, Caddie or Equipment Not During Search - opponent incurs one stroke penalty and replace ball (Rule 18-3b)

By Fellow-Competitor, Caddie or Equipment - no penalty and replace ball (Rule18-4)

By Another Ball - replace moved ball (Rule 18-5)

except any ball he has played at the hole being played and any small object, such as a coin or a tee, when used to mark the position of a ball or the extent of an area in which a ball is to be dropped. Equipment includes a golf cart, whether or not motorised. If such a cart is shared by two or more players, the cart and everything in it are deemed to be the equipment of the player whose ball is involved except that, when the cart is being moved by one of the players sharing it, the cart and everything in it are deemed to be that player's equipment.

Note: A ball played at the hole being played is equipment when it has been lifted and not put back into play.

A player has "addressed the ball" when he has taken his **stance** and has also grounded his club, except that in a **hazard** a player has addressed the ball when he has taken his stance.

Taking the "stance" consists in a player placing his feet in position for and preparatory to making a **stroke**.

RULE 18-1
BY OUTSIDE AGENCY

If a ball at rest is moved by an **outside agency**, the player shall incur no penalty and the ball shall be replaced before the player plays another **stroke**. (Player's ball at rest moved by another ball – see Rule 18-5.)

RULE 18-2
BY PLAYER, PARTNER, CADDIE OR EQUIPMENT

a *General*

When a player's ball is **in play**, if:

(i) the player, his partner or either of their caddies lifts or moves it, touches it purposely (except with a club in the act of addressing it) or causes it to move except as permitted by a Rule, or

(ii) equipment of the player or his partner causes the ball to move,

the player shall incur a penalty stroke. The ball shall be replaced unless the movement of the ball occurs after the player has begun his swing and he does not discontinue his swing.

Under the Rules no penalty is incurred if a player accidentally causes his ball to move in the following circumstances:

In measuring to determine which ball farther from hole – Rule 10-4
In searching for covered ball in **hazard** or for ball in **casual water**, **ground under repair**, etc. – Rule 12-1
In the process of repairing hole plug or ball mark Rule 16-1c
In the process of removing l**oose impediments** on **putting green** – Rule 18-2c
In the process of lifting ball under a Rule – Rule 20-1.
In the process of placing or replacing ball under a Rule – Rule 20-3a
In removal of movable **obstruction** – Rule 24-1

b *Ball Moving After Address*

If a player's **ball in play moves** after he has **addressed** it (other than as a result of a stroke), the player shall be deemed to have moved the ball and *shall incur a penalty stroke.* The player shall replace the ball unless the

53

movement of the ball occurs after he has begun his swing and he does not discontinue his swing.

c *Ball Moving After Loose Impediment*

Through the green, if the ball **moves** after any **loose impediment**, lying within a club-length of it has been touched by the player, his partner or either of their caddies and before the player has **addressed** it, the player shall be deemed to have moved the ball and *shall incur a penalty stroke*. The player shall replace the ball unless the movement of the ball occurs after he has begun his swing and he does not discontinue his swing.

On the **putting green**, if the ball or the ball-marker **moves** in the process of removing any **loose impediment**, the ball or the ball-marker shall be replaced. There is no penalty provided the movement of the ball or the ball-marker is directly attributable to the removal of the loose impediment. Otherwise, *the player shall incur a penalty stroke* under Rule 18-2a or 20-1

RULE 18-3

BY OPPONENT, CADDIE OR EQUIPMENT IN MATCH PLAY

a *During Search*

If, during search for a player's ball, the ball is moved by an opponent, his caddie or his **equipment**, no penalty is incurred and the player shall replace the ball.

b *Other Than During Search*

If, other than during search for a ball, the ball is touched or moved by an opponent, his caddie or his **equipment,** except as otherwise provided in the Rules, *the opponent shall incur a penalty stroke*. The player shall replace the ball.

(Ball moved in measuring to determine which ball farther from the hole – see Rule 10-4.)

(Playing a wrong ball – see Rule 15-2.)

RULE 18-4

BY FELLOW-COMPETITOR, CADDIE OR EQUIPMENT IN STROKE PLAY

If a competitor's ball is moved by a fellow-competitor, his caddie or his **equipment**, no penalty is incurred. The competitor shall replace his ball.

(Playing a wrong ball – see Rule 15-3.)

RULE 18-5

BY ANOTHER BALL

If a ball in play and at rest is moved by another ball in motion after a stroke, the moved ball shall be replaced.

PENALTY FOR BREACH OF RULE: *Match play – Loss of hole; Stroke play – Two strokes. If a player who is required to replace a ball fails to do so, he shall incur the general penalty for breach of Rule 18 but no additional penalty under Rule 18 shall be applied.*

Note 1: If a ball to be replaced under this Rule is not immediately recoverable, another ball may be substituted.

Note 2: If it is impossible to determine the spot on which a ball is to be placed, see Rule 20-3c.

19 BALL IN MOTION DEFLECTED OR STOPPED

DEFINITIONS

An "outside agency" is any agency not part of the match or, in stroke play, not part of the competitor's side, and includes a referee, a marker, an observer and a forecaddie. Neither wind nor water is an outside agency.

"Equipment" is anything used, worn or carried by or for the player except any ball he has played at the hole being played and any small object, such as a coin or a tee, when used to mark the position of a ball or the extent of an area in which a ball is to be dropped. Equipment includes a golf cart, whether or not motorised. If such a cart is shared by two or more players, the cart and everything in it are deemed to be the equipment of the player whose ball is involved except that, when the cart is being moved by one of the players sharing it, the cart and everything in it are deemed to be that player's equipment.

Note: A ball played at the hole being played is equipment when it has been lifted and not put back into play.

RULE 19-1
BY OUTSIDE AGENCY

If a ball in motion is accidentally deflected or stopped by any **outside agency**, it is a **rub of the green**, no penalty is incurred and the ball shall be played as it lies except:

a. If a ball in motion after a **stroke** other than on the **putting green** comes to rest in or on any moving or animate outside agency, the player shall, **through the green** or in a **hazard**, drop the ball, or on the putting green place the ball, as near as possible to the spot where the outside agency was when the ball came to rest in or on it, and

b. If a ball in motion after a stroke on the putting green is deflected or stopped by, or comes to rest in or on, any moving or animate outside agency except a worm or an insect, the stroke shall be cancelled, the ball replaced and the stroke replayed.

If the ball is not immediately recoverable, another ball may be substituted.(Player's ball deflected or stopped by another ball — see Rule 19-5.)

Note: If the referee or the Committee determines that a player's ball has been purposely deflected or stopped by an outside agency, Rule 1-4 applies to the player. If the **outside agency** is a fellow-competitor or his caddie, Rule 1-2 applies to the fellow-competitor.

RULE 19-2
BY PLAYER, PARTNER, CADDIE OR EQUIPMENT

a *Match Play*

If a player's ball is accidentally deflected or stopped by himself, his partner or either of their caddies or **equipment**, *he shall lose the hole.*

b *Stroke Play*

If a competitor's ball is accidentally deflected or stopped by himself, his partner or either of their caddies or equipment, *the competitor shall incur a*

BALL IN MOTION DEFLECTED OR STOPPED

By Player, Partner, Caddie or Equipment Match Play - player loses hole (Rule 19-2a)

By Player, Partner, Caddie or Equipment Stroke Play - player incurs penalty of two strokes and ball played as it lies (Rule 19-2b)

By Outside Agency - no penalty and ball played as it lies (Rule 19-1)

By Opponent, Caddie or Equipment Match Play - no penalty and ball played as it lies or stroke cancelled and replayed (Rule 19-3)

Stroke Play - see Rule 19-1 regarding ball deflected by Outside Agency (Rule 19-4)

By Another Ball at Rest - no penalty and ball played as it lies. Except in stroke play, if both balls lay on green prior to stroke, player incurs two stroke penalty (Rule 19-5a)

By Another Ball in Motion - no penalty and ball played as it lies, unless player in breach of Rule 16-1g (Rule 19-5b) *penalty of two strokes.* The ball shall be played as it lies, except when it comes to rest in or on the competitor's, his partner's or either of their caddies' clothes or equipment, in which case the competitor shall **through the green** or in a **hazard** drop the ball, or on the **putting green** place the ball, as near as possible to where the article was when the ball came to rest in or on it.

Exception: Dropped Ball – see Rule 20-2a. (Ball purposely deflected or stopped by player, partner or caddie – see Rule 1-2.)

RULE 19-3
BY OPPONENT, CADDIE OR EQUIPMENT IN MATCH PLAY

If a player's ball is accidentally deflected or stopped by an opponent, his caddie or his **equipment**, no penalty is incurred. The player may play the ball as it lies or, before another **stroke** is played by either side, cancel the stroke and play a ball without penalty as nearly as possible at the spot from which the original ball was last played (see Rule 20-5).

If the ball has come to rest in or on the opponent's or his caddie's clothes or equipment, the player may **through the green** or in a **hazard** drop the ball, or on the putting green place the ball, as near as possible to where the article was when the ball came to rest in or on it.

Exception: Ball striking person attending flagstick – see Rule 17-3b.

(Ball purposely deflected or stopped by opponent or caddie – see Rule 1-2.)

RULE 19-4
BY FELLOW-COMPETITOR, CADDIE OR EQUIPMENT IN STROKE PLAY

See Rule 19-1 regarding ball deflected by outside agency.

RULE 19-5
BY ANOTHER BALL

a *At Rest*

If a player's ball in motion after a stroke is deflected or stopped by a ball in play and at rest, the player shall play his ball as it lies.

In match play, no penalty is incurred. In stroke play, there is no penalty unless both balls lay on the **putting green** prior to the stroke, in which case *the player incurs a penalty of two strokes.*

b *In Motion*

If a player's ball in motion after a stroke is deflected or stopped by another ball in motion after a stroke, the player shall play his ball as it lies. There is no penalty unless the player was in breach of Rule 16-1g, in which case *he shall incur the penalty for breach of that Rule.*

Exception: If the player's ball is in motion after a stroke on the putting green and the other ball in motion is an outside agency – see Rule 19-1b.

PENALTY FOR BREACH OF RULE: *Match play – Loss of hole; Stroke play – Two strokes.*

PROCEDURE FOR LIFTING BALL

Although I want your ball lifted because it is interfering with my play, why are you marking it?

Because when a ball is lifted anywhere on the course and has to be replaced, its position must be marked.

20 | LIFTING, DROPPING AND PLACING; PLAYING FROM WRONG PLACE

RULE 20-1
LIFTING

A ball to be lifted under the Rules may be lifted by the player, his partner or another person authorised by the player. In any such case, the player shall be responsible for any breach of the Rules.

The position of the ball shall be marked before it is lifted under a Rule which requires it to be replaced. If it is not marked, *the player shall incur a penalty of one stroke* and the ball shall be replaced. If it is not replaced, *the player shall incur the general penalty* for breach of this Rule but no additional penalty under Rule 20-1 shall be applied.

If a ball or ball-marker is accidentally moved in the process of lifting the ball under a Rule or marking its position, the ball or the ball-marker shall be replaced. There is no penalty provided the movement of the ball or the ball-marker is directly attributable to the specific act of marking the position of or lifting the ball. Otherwise, *the player shall incur a penalty stroke* under this Rule or Rule 18-2a.

Exception: If a player incurs a penalty for failing to act in accordance with Rule 5-3 or 12-2, no additional penalty under Rule 20-1 shall be applied.

Note: The position of a ball to be lifted should be marked by placing a ball-marker, a small coin or other similar object immediately behind the ball. If the ball-marker interferes with the play, **stance** or **stroke** of another player, it should be placed one or more clubhead-lengths to one side.

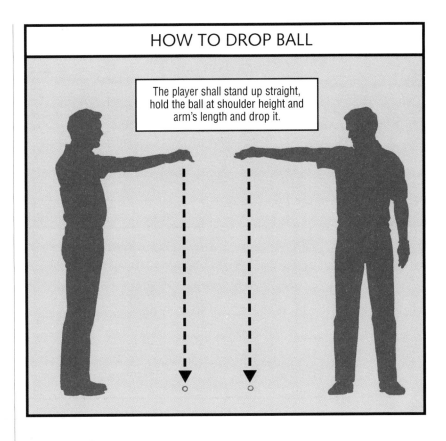

HOW TO DROP BALL

The player shall stand up straight, hold the ball at shoulder height and arm's length and drop it.

RULE 20-2
DROPPING AND RE-DROPPING

a *By Whom and How*

A ball to be dropped under the Rules shall be dropped by the player himself He shall stand erect, hold the ball at shoulder height and arm's length and drop it. If a ball is dropped by any other person or in any other manner and the error is not corrected as provided in Rule 20-6, *the player shall incur a penalty stroke.*

If the ball touches the player, his partner, either of their caddies or their equipment before or after it strikes a part of the course, the ball shall be re-dropped, without penalty. There is no limit to the number of times a ball shall be re-dropped in such circumstances.

(Taking action to influence position or movement of ball — see Rule 1-2.)

b *Where to Drop*

When a ball is to be dropped as near as possible to a specific spot, it shall be dropped not nearer the hole than the specific spot which, if it is not precisely known to the player, shall be estimated.

A ball when dropped must first strike a part of the course where the applicable Rule requires it to be dropped. If it is not so dropped, Rules 20-6 and -7 apply.

c *When to Re-Drop*

A dropped ball shall be re-dropped without penalty if it:
(i)   rolls into a **hazard**;
(ii)   rolls out of a hazard;
(iii)   rolls onto a **putting green**;

59

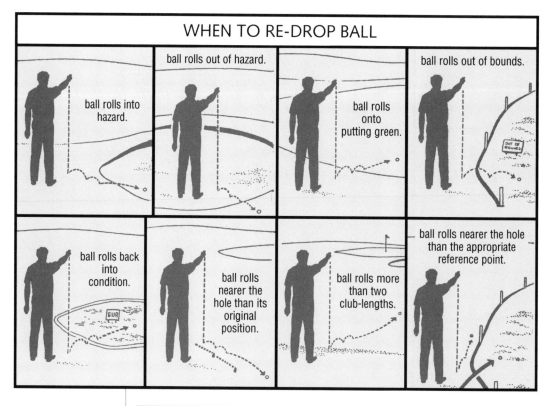

WHEN TO RE-DROP BALL

ball rolls into hazard.

ball rolls out of hazard.

ball rolls onto putting green.

ball rolls out of bounds.

ball rolls back into condition.

ball rolls nearer the hole than its original position.

ball rolls more than two club-lengths.

ball rolls nearer the hole than the appropriate reference point.

Your ball is going to be in my way. Will you please mark it?

OK, but first let's make sure we know what sort of lie I have got. If your shot alters my present lie I will have to recreate the lie as nearly as possible and place the ball in that lie.

(iv)   rolls **out of bounds**;

(v)   rolls to a position where there is interference by the condition from which relief was taken under Rule 24-2 (immovable obstruction) or Rule 25-1 (abnormal ground conditions), or rolls back into the pitch-mark from which it was lifted under Rule 25-2 (embedded ball);

(vi)   rolls and comes to rest more than two club-lengths from where it first struck a part of the course; or

(vii) rolls and comes to rest nearer the hole than its original position or

estimated position (see Rule 20-2b) unless otherwise permitted by the Rules.

(viii)   rolls and comes to rest nearer the hole than the point where the original ball last crossed the margin of the area or hazard, (Rule 25-1c(i) and (ii))   or the margin of the water hazard (Rule 26-1b) or lateral water hazard (Rule 26-1c).

If the ball when re-dropped rolls into any position listed above, it shall be placed as near as possible to the spot where it first struck a part of the course when re-dropped.

If a ball to be re-dropped or placed under this Rule is not immediately recoverable, another ball may be substituted.

RULE 20-3
PLACING AND REPLACING

a *By Whom and Where*

A ball to be placed under the Rules shall be placed by the player or his partner. If a ball is to be replaced, the player, his partner or the person who lifted or moved it shall place it on the spot from which it was lifted or moved. In any such case, the player shall be responsible for any breach of the Rules. If a ball or ball-marker is accidentally moved in the process of placing or replacing the ball, the ball or the ball-marker shall be replaced. There is no penalty provided the movement of the ball or the ball-marker is directly attributable to the specific act of placing or replacing the ball or removing the ball-marker. Otherwise, *the player shall incur a penalty stroke* under Rule 18-2a or 20-1.

61

b *Lie of Ball to be Placed or Replaced Altered*

If the original lie of a ball to be placed or replaced has been altered:

(i)   except in a **hazard**, the ball shall be placed in the nearest lie most similar to the original lie which is not more than one club-length from the original lie, not nearer the hole and not in a hazard;

(ii)   in a **water hazard**, the ball shall be placed in accordance with Clause (i) above, except that the ball must be placed in the water hazard;

(iii)   in a **bunker**, the original lie shall be recreated as nearly as possible and the ball shall be placed in that lie.

c *Spot Not Determinable*

If it is impossible to determine the spot where the ball is to be placed or replaced:

(i)   **through the green**, the ball shall be dropped as near as possible to the place where it lay but not in a **hazard** or on a **putting green**;

(ii)   in a hazard, the ball shall be dropped in the hazard as near as possible to the place where it lay;

(iii)   on the putting green, the ball shall be placed as near as possible to the place where it lay but not in a hazard.

d *Ball Fails to Come to Rest on Spot*

If a ball when placed fails to come to rest on the spot on which it was placed, it shall be replaced without penalty. If it still fails to come to rest on that spot:

(i)   except in a **hazard,** it shall be placed at the nearest spot not nearer the hole or in a hazard where it can be placed at rest;

(ii)   in a hazard, it shall be placed in the hazard at the nearest spot not nearer the hole where it can be placed at rest.

   If a ball when placed comes to rest on the spot on which it is placed, and it subsequently moves, there is no penalty and the ball shall be played as it lies, unless the provisions of any other Rule apply.

PENALTY FOR BREACH OF RULE 20-1, -2 or -3: *Match play – Loss of hole; Stroke play – Two strokes.*

RULE 20-4
WHEN BALL DROPPED OR PLACED IS IN PLAY

If the player's **ball in play** has been lifted, it is again in play when dropped or placed.

   A substituted ball becomes the ball in play when it has been dropped or placed.

(Ball incorrectly substituted – see Rule 15-1).

(Lifting ball incorrectly substituted, dropped or placed – see Rule 20-6).

RULE 20-5
PLAYING NEXT STROKE FROM WHERE PREVIOUS STROKE PLAYED

When, under the Rules, a player elects or is required to play his next **stroke** from where a previous stroke was played, he shall proceed as follows: if the stroke is to be played from the **teeing ground**, the ball to be played shall be played from anywhere within the teeing ground and may be teed; if the stroke is to be played from **through the green** or a **hazard**, it shall be dropped; if the stroke is to be played on the **putting green**, it shall be placed.

PENALTY FOR BREACH OF RULE 20-5: *Match play – Loss of hole; Stroke play – Two strokes.*

RULE 20-6
LIFTING BALL INCORRECTLY SUBSTITUTED, DROPPED OR PLACED

A ball incorrectly substituted, dropped or placed in a wrong place or otherwise not in accordance with the Rules but not played may be lifted, without penalty, and the player shall then proceed correctly.

RULE 20-7
PLAYING FROM WRONG PLACE

For a ball played from outside the teeing ground or from a wrong teeing ground – see Rule 11-4 and -5.

a *Match Play*

If a player plays a stroke with a ball which has been dropped or placed in a wrong place, *he shall lose the hole.*

b *Stroke Play*

If a competitor plays a stroke with his **ball in play** (i) which has been dropped or placed in a wrong place or (ii) which has been moved and not replaced in a case where the Rules require replacement, *he shall*, provided a serious breach has not occurred, *incur the penalty prescribed by the applicable Rule* and play out the hole with the ball.

If, after playing from a wrong place, a competitor becomes aware of

PLAYING FROM WRONG PLACE

If a player moves his ball-marker a putter head length to one side, he must remember to put it back before he putts. Otherwise, the player will be penalised for playing from a wrong place.

that fact and believes that a serious breach may be involved, he may, provided he has not played a stroke from the next teeing ground or, in the case of the last hole of the round, left the putting green, declare that he will play out the hole with a second ball dropped or placed in accordance with the Rules. The competitor shall report the facts to the Committee before returning his score card; if he fails to do so, *he shall be disqualified.* The Committee shall determine whether a serious breach of the Rule occurred. If so, the score with the second ball shall count and *the competitor shall add two penalty strokes to his score with that ball.*

If a serious breach has occurred and the competitor has failed to correct it as prescribed above, *he shall be disqualified.*

Note: If a competitor plays a second ball, penalty strokes incurred by playing the ball ruled not to count and strokes subsequently taken with that ball shall be disregarded.

21 CLEANING BALL

A ball on the putting green may be cleaned when lifted under Rule l6-1b. Elsewhere, a ball may be cleaned when lifted except when it has been lifted:

a. To determine if it is unfit for play (Rule 5-3);

b. For identification (Rule 12-2), in which case it may be cleaned only to the extent necessary for identification; or

c. Because it is interfering with or assisting play (Rule 22).

If a player cleans his ball during play of a hole except as provided in this Rule, *he shall incur a penalty of one stroke* and the ball, if lifted, shall be replaced.

If a player who is required to replace a ball fails to do so, *he shall incur the penalty* for breach of Rule 20-3a, but no additional penalty under Rule 21 shall be applied.

Exception: If a player incurs a penalty for failing to act in accordance with Rule 5-3, 12-2 or 22, no additional penalty under Rule 21 shall be applied.

22 BALL INTERFERING WITH OR ASSISTING PLAY

Any player may:

a. Lift his ball if he considers that the ball might assist any other player or

b. Have any other ball lifted if he considers that the ball might interfere with his play or assist the play of any other player,

but this may not be done while another ball is in motion. In stroke play, a player required to lift his ball may play first rather than lift. A ball lifted under this Rule shall be replaced.

PENALTY FOR BREACH OF RULE: *Match play – Loss of hole; Stroke play – Two strokes.*

BALL INTERFERING WITH OR ASSISTING PLAY

Note: Except on the putting green, the ball may not be cleaned when lifted under this Rule – see Rule 21.

23 LOOSE IMPEDIMENTS

DEFINITIONS

"Loose impediments" are natural objects such as stones, leaves, twigs, branches and the like, dung, worms and insects and casts or heaps made by them, provided they are not fixed or growing, are not solidly embedded and do not adhere to the ball.

*Sand and loose soil are loose impediments on the **putting green** but not elsewhere.*

*Snow and natural ice, other than frost, are either **casual water** or loose impediments, at the option of the player. Manufactured ice is an **obstruction**.*

Dew and frost are not loose impediments.

RULE 23-1
RELIEF

Except when both the **loose impediment** and the ball lie in or touch the same **hazard**, any loose impediment may be removed without penalty. If the ball moves, see Rule 18-2c.

When a ball is in motion, a loose impediment which might influence the movement of the ball shall not be removed.

PENALTY FOR BREACH OF RULE: *Match play – Loss of hole; Stroke play – Two strokes.*
(Searching for ball in hazard — see Rule 12-1.)
(Touching line of putt — see Rule 16-1a.)

24 OBSTRUCTIONS

DEFINITION

An "obstruction" is anything artificial, including the artificial surfaces and sides of roads and paths and manufactured ice, except:
a. *Objects defining* **out of bounds**, *such as walls, fences, stakes and railings;*
b. *Any part of an immovable artificial object which is out of bounds; and* **c.** *Any construction declared by the Committee to be an integral part of the course.*

RULE 24-1
MOVABLE OBSTRUCTION

A player may obtain relief from a movable **obstruction** as follows:
a. If the ball does not lie in or on the obstruction, the obstruction may be removed. If the ball moves, it shall be replaced, and there is no penalty provided that the movement of the ball is directly attributable to the removal of the obstruction. Otherwise, Rule 18-2a applies.
b. If the ball lies in or on the obstruction, the ball may be lifted, without penalty, and the obstruction removed. The ball shall **through the green** or in

BALL RESTING AGAINST RAKE ROLLS INTO BUNKER WHEN REMOVED

If I move the rake my ball is likely to roll into the bunker. If it does, may I replace it?

Yes, and if it will not come to rest on the correct spot when replaced, you may place it at the nearest spot, not nearer the hole or in the bunker, where it can be placed at rest.

Note: It is recommended that rakes be placed outside bunkers, as far away from the bunkers as is practical and in positions where they will be least likely to affect play.

ROADS AND PATHS

BALL BEHIND IMMOVABLE OBSTRUCTION

IMMOVABLE OBSTRUCTION

RELIEF FROM OBSTRUCTION GIVES RELIEF FOR LINE OF PLAY

STILE IN BOUNDARY FENCE

NO RELIEF WITHOUT PENALTY IN WATER HAZARD

69

a **hazard** be dropped, or on the **putting green** be placed, as near as possible to the spot directly under the place where the ball lay in or on the obstruction, but not nearer the hole.

The ball may be cleaned when lifted under Rule 24-1.

When a ball is in motion, an obstruction which might influence the movement of the ball, other than an attended flagstick or equipment of the players, shall not be removed.

Note: If a ball to be dropped or placed under this Rule is not immediately recoverable, another ball may be substituted.

RULE 24-2
IMMOVABLE OBSTRUCTION

a *Interference*

Interference by an immovable **obstruction** occurs when a ball lies in or on the obstruction, or so close to the obstruction that the obstruction interferes with the player's **stance** or the area of his intended swing. If the player's ball lies on the **putting green**, interference also occurs if an immovable obstruction on the putting green intervenes on his line of putt. Otherwise, intervention on the line of play is not, of itself, interference under this Rule.

b *Relief*

Except when the ball is in a **water hazard** or a **lateral water hazard**, a player may obtain relief from interference by an immovable obstruction, without penalty, as follows:

(i)   **Through the Green:** if the ball lies **through the green**, the point on the **course** nearest to where the ball lies shall be determined (without crossing over, through or under the obstruction) which (a) is not nearer the hole, (b) avoids interference (as defined) and (c) is not in a **hazard** or on a **putting green**. The player shall lift the ball and drop it within one club-length of the point thus determined on a part of the course which fulfils (a), (b) and (c) above.

Note: The prohibition against crossing over, through or under the **obstruction** does not apply to the artificial surfaces and sides of roads and paths or when the ball lies in or on the obstruction.

(ii)   **In a Bunker:** If the ball is in a **bunker**, the player shall lift and drop the ball in accordance with Clause (i) above, except that the ball must be dropped in the bunker.

(iii)   **On the Putting Green:** If the ball lies on the **putting green,** the player shall lift the ball and place it in the nearest position to where it lay which affords relief from interference, but not nearer the hole nor in a hazard.

The ball may be cleaned when lifted under Rule 24-2b.

(Ball rolling to a position where there is interference by the condition from which relief was taken – *see* Rule 20-2c(v).)

Exception: A player may not obtain relief under Rule 24-2b if

(a) it is clearly unreasonable for him to play a stroke because of interference by anything other than an immovable obstruction or

(b) interference by an immovable obstruction would occur only through use of an unnecessarily abnormal stance, swing or direction of play.

Note 1: If a ball is in a **water hazard** (including a **lateral water hazard**), the player is not entitled to relief without penalty from interference by an immovable obstruction. The player shall play the ball as it lies or proceed under Rule 26-1.

Note 2: If a ball to be dropped or placed under this Rule is not immediately recoverable, another ball may be substituted.

c *Ball Lost*

Except in a **water hazard** or a **lateral water hazard**, if there is reasonable evidence that a ball is lost in an immovable obstruction, the player may, without penalty, substitute another ball and follow the procedure prescribed in Rule 24-2b. For the purpose of applying this Rule, the ball shall be deemed to lie at the spot where it entered the obstruction. If the ball is lost in an underground drain pipe or culvert the entrance to which is in a **hazard**, a ball must be dropped in that hazard or the player may proceed under Rule 26-1, if applicable.

PENALTY FOR BREACH OF RULE: *Match Play – Loss of hole; Stroke play – Two strokes.*

25 ABNORMAL GROUND CONDITIONS AND WRONG PUTTING GREEN

DEFINITIONS

"Casual water" is any temporary accumulation of water on the **course** *which is visible before or after the player takes his* **stance** *and is not in a* **water hazard.** *Snow and natural ice, other than frost, are either casual water or* loose impediments, *at the option of the player. Manufactured ice is an* **obstruction.** *Dew and frost are not casual water. A ball is in casual water when it lies in or any part of it touches the casual water.*

"Ground under repair" is any portion of the **course** *so marked by order of the Committee or so declared by its authorised representative. It includes material piled for removal and a hole made by a greenkeeper, even if not so marked. Stakes and lines defining ground under repair are in such ground. Stakes defining ground under repair are obstructions. The margin of ground under repair extends vertically downwards, but not upwards. A ball is in ground under repair when it lies in or any part of it touches the ground under repair.*

Note 1: Grass cuttings and other material left on the course which have been abandoned and are not intended to be removed are not ground under repair unless so marked.

Note 2: The Committee may make a Local Rule prohibiting play from ground under repair or an environmentally-sensitive area which has been defined as ground under repair.

RULE 25-1
CASUAL WATER, GROUND UNDER REPAIR AND CERTAIN DAMAGE TO COURSE

a *Interference*

Interference by **casual water**, **ground under repair** or a hole, cast or runway made by a burrowing animal, a reptile or a bird occurs when a ball lies in or touches any of these conditions or when such a condition on the **course**

GROUND UNDER REPAIR: EXAMPLES

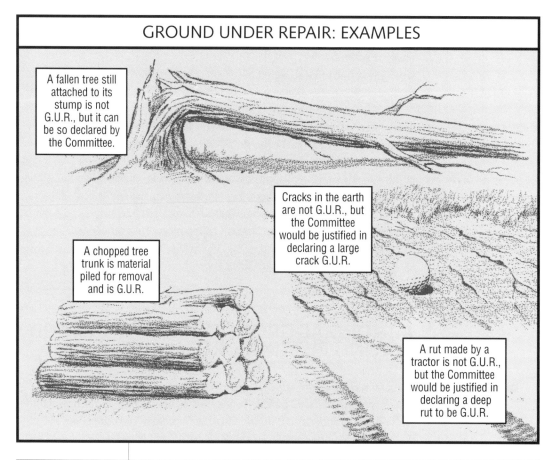

A fallen tree still attached to its stump is not G.U.R., but it can be so declared by the Committee.

Cracks in the earth are not G.U.R., but the Committee would be justified in declaring a large crack G.U.R.

A chopped tree trunk is material piled for removal and is G.U.R.

A rut made by a tractor is not G.U.R., but the Committee would be justified in declaring a deep rut to be G.U.R.

AREAS REQUIRING PRESERVATION

If there is an area of the course, such as a plantation of young trees, which requires preservation the Committee should declare it "Ground Under Repair - Play Prohibited".

interferes with the player's **stance** or the area of his intended swing.

If the player's ball lies on the **putting green**, interference also occurs if such condition on the putting green intervenes on his line of putt.

If interference exists, the player may either play the ball as it lies (unless prohibited by Local Rule) or take relief as provided in Clause b.

Note: The Committee may make a Local Rule denying the player relief from interference with his stance by all or any of the conditions covered by this Rule.

b *Relief*

If the player elects to take relief, he shall proceed as follows:

(i) **Through the Green:** If the ball lies **through the green**, the point on the **course** nearest to where the ball lies shall be determined which (a) is not nearer the hole, (b) avoids interference by the condition, and (c) is not in a **hazard** or on a **putting green**. The player shall lift the ball and drop it without penalty within one club-length of the point thus determined on a part of the course which fulfils (a), (b) and (c) above.

(ii) **In a Hazard:** If the ball is in a **hazard**, the player shall lift and drop the ball either:
(a) Without penalty, in the hazard, as near as possible to the spot where the ball lay, but not nearer the hole, on a part of the course which affords maximum available relief from the condition; or (b) *Under penalty of one stroke,* outside the hazard, keeping the point where the ball lay directly between the hole and the spot on which the ball is dropped, with no limit to how far behind the hazard the ball may be dropped.

Exception: If a ball is in a **water hazard** (including a **lateral water hazard**), the player is not entitled to relief without penalty from a hole, cast or runway made by a burrowing animal, a reptile or a bird. The player shall play the ball as it lies or proceed under Rule 26-1.

(iii) **On the Putting Green:** If the ball lies on the **putting green,** the player shall lift the ball and place it without penalty in the nearest position to where it lay which affords maximum available relief from the condition, but not nearer the hole nor in a hazard.

The ball may be cleaned when lifted under Rule 25-1b.

(Ball rolling to a position where there is interference by the condition from which relief was taken — see Rule 20-2c(v).)

Exception: A player may not obtain relief under Rule 25-1b if (a) it is clearly unreasonable for him to play a stroke because of interference by anything other than a condition covered by Rule 25-1a or (b) interference by such a condition would occur only through use of an unnecessarily abnormal stance, swing or direction of play.

Note: If a ball to be dropped or placed under this Rule is not immediately recoverable, another ball may be substituted.

c *Ball Lost Under Condition Covered by Rule 25-1*

It is a question of fact whether a ball lost after having been struck toward a condition covered by Rule 25-1 is lost under such condition. In order to treat the ball as lost under such condition, there must be reasonable evidence to that effect. In the absence of such evidence, the ball must be treated as a

CASUAL WATER ON PUTTING GREEN

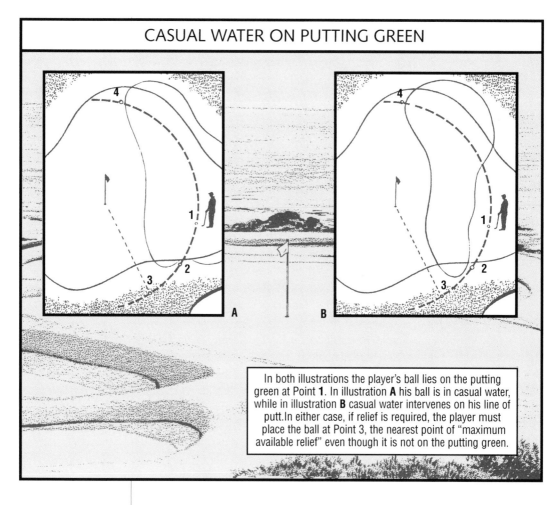

In both illustrations the player's ball lies on the putting green at Point **1**. In illustration **A** his ball is in casual water, while in illustration **B** casual water intervenes on his line of putt. In either case, if relief is required, the player must place the ball at Point 3, the nearest point of "maximum available relief" even though it is not on the putting green.

lost ball and Rule 27 applies.

(i) **Outside a Hazard:** If a ball is lost outside a **hazard** under a condition covered by Rule 25-1, the player may take relief as follows: the point on the **course** nearest to where the ball last crossed the margin of the area shall be determined which (a) is not nearer the hole than where the ball last crossed the margin, (b) avoids interference by the condition and (c) is not in a hazard or on a **putting green**. He shall drop a ball without penalty within one club-length of the point thus determined on a part of the course which fulfils (a), (b) and (c) above.

(ii) **In a Hazard:** If a ball is lost in a **hazard** under a condition covered by Rule 25-1, the player may drop a ball either:

(a) Without penalty, in the hazard, as near as possible to the point at which the original ball last crossed the margin of the area, but not nearer the hole, on a part of the course which affords maximum available relief from the condition; or

(b) *Under penalty of one stroke,* outside the hazard, keeping the point at which the original ball last crossed the margin of the hazard directly between the hole and the spot on which the ball is dropped, with no limit to how far behind the hazard the ball may be dropped.

Exception: If a ball is in a **water hazard** (including a **lateral water hazard**), the

BALL CLOSE TO CASUAL WATER: LEFT HANDED STROKE NOT REASONABLE

BALL CLOSE TO CASUAL WATER: LEFT HANDED STROKE REASONABLE

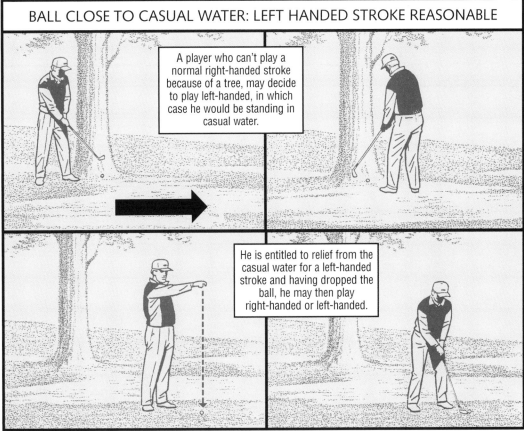

STANCE INTERFERED WITH BY BURROWING ANIMAL HOLE: BALL UNPLAYABLE BECAUSE OF OTHER CONDITION

EMBEDDED BALL

player is not entitled to relief without penalty for a ball lost in a hole, cast or runway made by a burrowing animal, a reptile or a bird. The player shall proceed under Rule 26-1.

RULE 25-2
EMBEDDED BALL

A ball embedded in its own pitch-mark in the ground in any closely-mown area **through the green** may be lifted, cleaned and dropped, without penalty, as near as possible to the spot where it lay but not nearer the hole. The ball when dropped must first strike a part of the course through the green. "Closely-mown area" means any area of the **course**, including paths through the rough, cut to fairway height or less.

RULE 25-3
WRONG PUTTING GREEN

A player must not play a ball which lies on a **putting green** other than that of the hole being played. The ball must be lifted and the player must proceed as follows: The point on the course nearest to where the ball lies shall be determined which (a) is not nearer the hole and (b) is not in a **hazard** or on a putting green. The player shall lift the ball and drop it without penalty within one club-length of the point thus determined on a part of the course which fulfils (a) and (b) above. The ball may be cleaned when so lifted.

Note: Unless otherwise prescribed by the Committee, the term "a putting green other than that of the hole being played" includes a practice putting green or pitching green on the course.

PENALTY FOR BREACH OF RULE: *Match play – Loss of hole; Stroke play – Two strokes*

26 WATER HAZARDS (INCLUDING LATERAL WATER HAZARDS)

DEFINITIONS

A "water hazard" is any sea, lake, pond, river, ditch, surface drainage ditch or other open water course (whether or not containing water) and anything of a similar nature.

All ground or water within the margin of a water hazard is part of the water hazard. The margin of a water hazard extends vertically upwards and downwards. Stakes and lines defining the margins of water hazards are in the hazards. Such stakes are obstructions. A ball is in a water hazard when it lies in or any part of it touches the water hazard.

Note 1: Water hazards (other than **lateral water hazards**) should be defined by yellow stakes or lines.

Note 2: The Committee may make a Local Rule prohibiting play from an environmentally-sensitive area which has been defined as a water hazard.

A "lateral water hazard" is a water **hazard** or that part of a water hazard so situated that it is not possible or is deemed by the Committee to be impracticable to drop a ball behind the water hazard in accordance with Rule 26-1b.

REASONABLE EVIDENCE BALL IN WATER HAZARD

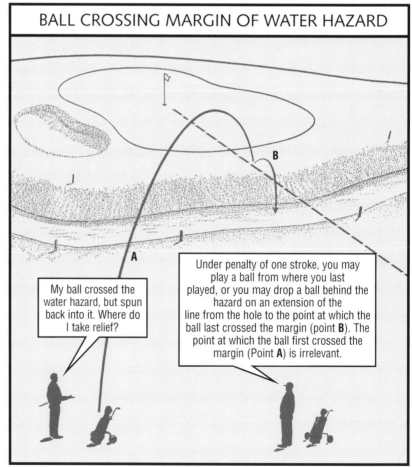

BALL CROSSING MARGIN OF WATER HAZARD

That part of a water hazard to be played as a lateral water hazard should be distinctively marked. A ball is in a lateral water hazard when it lies in or any part of it touches the lateral water hazard.
Note 1: Lateral water hazards should be defined by red stakes or lines.
Note 2: The Committee may make a Local Rule prohibiting play from an environmentally-sensitive area which has been defined as a lateral water hazard.

RULE 26-1
BALL IN WATER HAZARD

It is a question of fact whether a ball lost after having been struck towards a **water hazard** is lost inside or outside the hazard. In order to treat the ball as lost in the hazard, there must be reasonable evidence that the ball lodged in it. In the absence of such evidence, the ball must be treated as a lost ball and Rule 27 applies.

If a ball is in or is lost in a water hazard (whether the ball lies in water or not), the player may *under penalty of one stroke:*
a. Play a ball as nearly as possible at the spot from which the original ball was last played (see Rule 20-5); or
b. Drop a ball behind the water hazard, keeping the point at which the original ball last crossed the margin of the water hazard directly between the hole and the spot on which the ball is dropped, with no limit to how far behind the water hazard the ball may be dropped; or
c. *As additional options available only if the ball last crossed the margin of a lateral water hazard,* drop a ball outside the water hazard within two club-lengths of and not nearer the hole than (i) the point where the original ball last crossed the margin of the water hazard or (ii) a point on the opposite margin of the water hazard equidistant from the hole.

The ball may be cleaned when lifted under this Rule.
(Ball moving in water in a water hazard — see Rule 14-6.)

RULE 26-2
BALL PLAYED WITHIN WATER HAZARD

a *Ball Comes to Rest in the Hazard*

If a ball played from within a water hazard comes to rest in the same hazard after the stroke, the player may:
(i)   proceed under Rule 26-1; or.
(ii)   *under penalty of one stroke*, play a ball as nearly as possible at the spot from which the last stroke from outside the hazard was played (see Rule 20-5).

If the player proceeds under Rule 26-1a, he may elect not to play the dropped ball. If he so elects, he may:
(a) proceed under Rule 26-1b, *adding the additional penalty of one stroke* prescribed by that Rule; or
(b) proceed under Rule 26-1c, if applicable, *adding the additional penalty of one stroke* prescribed by that Rule; or
(c) *add an additional penalty of one stroke* and play a ball as nearly as possible at the spot from which the last stroke from outside the hazard was played (see Rule 20-5).

79

RELIEF FROM LATERAL WATER HAZARD

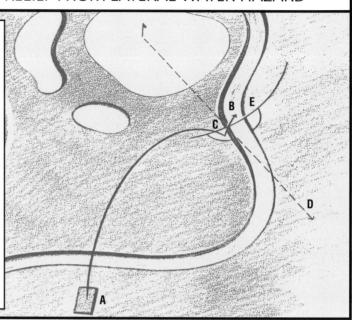

The player has played a ball from the tee (Point **A**) into the lateral water hazard at Point **B**. It last crossed the margin of the hazard at Point **C** and the point on the opposite margin, equidistant from the hole is Point **E**. He may play the ball as it lies or, under penalty of one stroke;
(i) play another ball from the tee - Rule 26-1a;
(ii) drop a ball anywhere on the far side of the hazard on the dotted line from the hole through Point **C**, e.g. Point **D** - Rule 26-1b;
(iii) drop a ball in the area on the near side of the hazard which is all ground within two club-lengths of Point **C** - Rule 26-1c(i); or
(iv) drop a ball in the area on the far side of the hazard which is all ground within two club-lengths of Point **E** - Rule 26-1c(ii)

b *Ball Lost or Unplayable Outside Hazard or Out of Bounds*

If a ball played from within a water hazard is lost or declared unplayable outside the hazard or is out of bounds, the player, after taking *a penalty of one stroke* under Rule 27-1 or 28a, may:

(i) play a ball as nearly as possible at the spot in the hazard from which the original ball was last played (see Rule 20-5); or

(ii) proceed under Rule 26-1b, or if applicable Rule 26-1c, *adding the additional penalty of one stroke* prescribed by the Rule and using as

BALL PLAYED FROM WITHIN WATER HAZARD

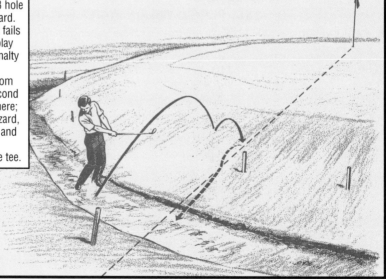

The player's tee shot at a par 3 hole comes to rest in a water hazard. He plays from the hazard, but fails to get his ball out. He may play the ball as it lies or, under penalty of one stroke:
(i) drop a ball at the spot from which he's just played his second stroke and play again from there;
(ii) drop a ball behind the hazard, anywhere on the dotted line, and play from there; or
(iii) play another ball from the tee.

the reference point the point where the original ball last crossed the margin of the hazard before it came to rest in the hazard; or

(iii) *add an additional penalty of one stroke* and play a ball as nearly as possible at the spot from which the last stroke from outside the hazard was played (see Rule 20-5).

Note 1: When proceeding under Rule 26-2b, the player is not required to drop a ball under Rule 27-1 or 28a. If he does drop a ball, he is not required to play it. He may alternatively proceed under Clause (ii) or (iii).

Note 2: If a ball played from within a water hazard is declared unplayable outside the hazard, nothing in Rule 26-2b precludes the player from proceeding under Rule 28b or c.

PENALTY FOR BREACH OF RULE: *Match play – Loss of hole; Stroke play – Two strokes.*

27 | BALL LOST OR OUT OF BOUNDS; PROVISIONAL BALL

DEFINITIONS *If the original ball is lost in an immovable obstruction (Rule 24-2) or under a condition covered by Rule 25-1 (casual water, ground under repair and certain damage to the course), the player may proceed under the applicable Rule. If the original ball is lost in a water hazard, the player shall proceed under Rule 26.*

Such Rules may not be used unless there is reasonable evidence that the ball is lost in an immovable obstruction, under a condition covered by Rule 25-1 or in a water hazard.

PLAYERS UNABLE TO IDENTIFY THEIR BALLS

BALL FOUND WITHIN FIVE MINUTES

A ball is "lost" if:

a. *It is not found or identified as his by the player within five minutes after the player's side or his or their caddies have begun to search for it; or*

b. *The player has put another ball into play under the Rules, even though he may not have searched for the original ball; or*

c. *The player has played any stroke with a* **provisional ball** *from the place where the original ball is likely to be or from a point nearer the hole than that place, whereupon the provisional ball becomes the* ball **in play**.

Time spent in playing a **wrong ball** *is not counted in the five-minute period allowed for search.*

"Out of bounds" is ground on which play is prohibited.

When out of bounds is defined by reference to stakes or a fence, or as being beyond stakes or a fence, the out of bounds line is determined by the nearest inside points of the stakes or fence posts at ground level, excluding angled supports.

When out of bounds is defined by a line on the ground, the line itself is out of bounds.

The out of bounds line extends vertically upwards and downwards.

A ball is out of bounds when all of it lies out of bounds.

A player may stand out of bounds to play a ball lying within bounds.

A "provisional ball" is a ball played under Rule 27-2 for a ball which may be **lost** *outside a* **water hazard** *or may be out of* **bounds**.

RULE 27-1
BALL LOST OR OUT OF BOUNDS

If a ball is **lost** outside a **water hazard** or is **out of bounds**, the player shall play a ball, *under penalty of one stroke*, as near as possible at the spot from which the original ball was last played (see Rule 20-5)

PENALTY FOR BREACH OF RULE 27-1: *Match Play – Loss of hole; Stroke Play – Two Strokes.*

RULE 27-2
PROVISIONAL BALL

a *Procedure*

If a ball may be **lost** outside a **water hazard** or may be **out of bounds**, to save time the player may play another ball provisionally as nearly as possible at the spot from which the original ball was played (see Rule 20-5). The player shall inform his opponent in match play or his marker or a fellow-competitor in stroke play that he intends to play a **provisional ball,** and he shall play it before he or his partner goes forward to search for the original ball. If he fails to do so and plays another ball, such ball is not a provisional ball and becomes the **ball in play** *under penalty of stroke and distance* (Rule 27-1); the original ball is deemed to be lost.

b *When Provisional Ball Becomes Ball in Play*

The player may play a provisional ball until he reaches the place where the original ball is likely to be. If he plays a stroke with the provisional ball from the place where the original ball is likely to be or from a point nearer the hole than that place, the original ball is deemed to be **lost** and the provisional ball becomes the ball in play under *penalty of stroke and distance* (Rule 27-1).

PROVISIONAL BALL BECOMES BALL IN PLAY

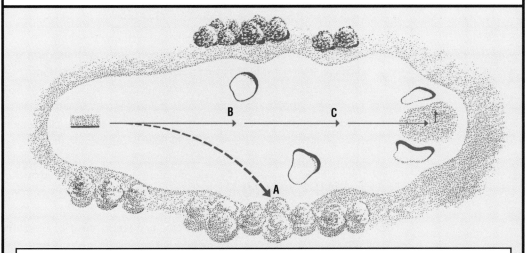

The player has played from the tee and his ball may be lost at **A**. He plays a provisional ball to **B** and then from **B** to **C**. The player decides not to look for his original ball at **A** and plays his provisional ball from **C** to the green. Consequently, the provisional ball becomes the ball in play, under penalty of stroke and distance and the original ball is by definition lost. This is because the player has played a stroke with the provisional ball from a point nearer the hole than the place where the original ball is likely to be.

PROVISIONAL BALL PLAYED: ORIGINAL BALL FOUND UNPLAYABLE

A player plays a provisional ball as his ball may be lost. The original ball is found within five minutes and before the provisional ball has become the ball in play, but the ball is unplayable. The player must abandon the provisional ball and proceed with the original ball.

If the original ball is lost outside a water hazard or is out of bounds, the provisional ball becomes the ball in play, *under penalty of stroke and distance* (Rule 27-1).

c *When Provisional Ball to Be Abandoned*

If the original ball is neither lost outside a water hazard nor out of bounds, the player shall abandon the provisional ball and continue play with the original ball. If he fails to do so, any further strokes played with the provisional ball shall constitute playing a **wrong ball** and the provisions of Rule 15 shall apply.

Note: If the original ball is in a water hazard, the player shall play the ball as it lies or proceed under Rule 26. If it is lost in a water hazard or unplayable, the player shall proceed under Rule 26 or 28, whichever is applicable.

28 BALL UNPLAYABLE

The player may declare his ball unplayable at any place on the course except when the ball is in a **water hazard**. The player is the sole judge as to whether his ball is unplayable.

If the player deems his ball to be unplayable, he shall, *under penalty of one stroke:*

a. Play a ball as nearly as possible at the spot from which the original ball was last played (see Rule 20-5); or

BALL UNPLAYABLE IN BUNKER: PLAYER'S OPTIONS

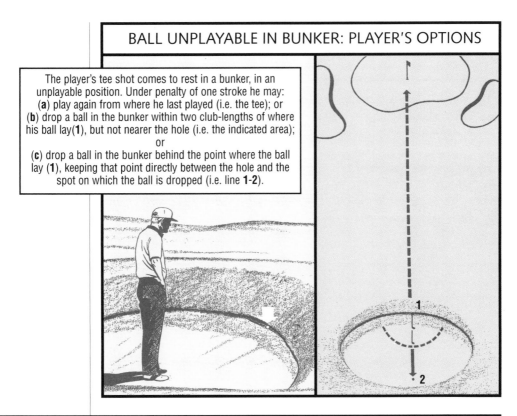

The player's tee shot comes to rest in a bunker, in an unplayable position. Under penalty of one stroke he may:
(**a**) play again from where he last played (i.e. the tee); or
(**b**) drop a ball in the bunker within two club-lengths of where his ball lay(**1**), but not nearer the hole (i.e. the indicated area); or
(**c**) drop a ball in the bunker behind the point where the ball lay (**1**), keeping that point directly between the hole and the spot on which the ball is dropped (i.e. line **1-2**).

BALL UNPLAYABLE IN BUSH: PLACE FOR DROPPING

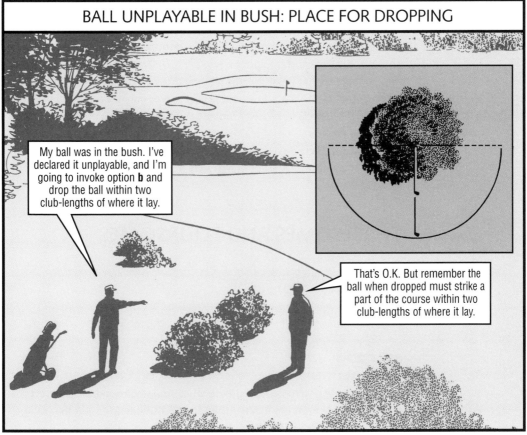

My ball was in the bush. I've declared it unplayable, and I'm going to invoke option **b** and drop the ball within two club-lengths of where it lay.

That's O.K. But remember the ball when dropped must strike a part of the course within two club-lengths of where it lay.

BALL DEEMED UNPLAYABLE

b. Drop a ball within two club-lengths of the spot where the ball lay, but not nearer the hole; or

c. Drop a ball behind the point where the ball lay, keeping that point directly between the hole and the spot on which the ball is dropped, with no limit to how far behind that point the ball may be dropped.

If the unplayable ball is in a **bunker**, the player may proceed under Clause a, b or c. If he elects to proceed under Clause b or c, a ball must be dropped in the bunker.

The ball may be cleaned when lifted under this Rule.

PENALTY FOR BREACH OF RULE: *Match play – Loss of hole; Stroke play – Two strokes.*

29 THREESOMES AND FOURSOMES

DEFINITIONS

Threesome: A match in which one plays against two, and each side plays one ball.
Foursome: A match in which two play against two, and each side plays one ball.

RULE 29-1
GENERAL

In a threesome or a foursome, during any **stipulated round** the partners shall play alternately from the teeing grounds and alternately during the play of each hole. **Penalty strokes** do not affect the order of play.

FOURSOMES: ORDER OF PLAY WHEN PARTNER DRIVES OUT OF BOUNDS

FOURSOMES : WHICH PARTNER DROPS BALL

ORDER OF PLAY IN 36-HOLE COMPETITION

Now that we're starting the second 18 holes, are we allowed to change the order of teeing off so that you drive at the evens and I drive at the odds?

Yes, unless the Committee in charge of the competition has laid down a condition to the contrary.

Rule 29-1. See Definition of Stipulated Round

RULE 29-2
MATCH PLAY

If a player plays when his partner should have played, *his side shall lose the hole*

RULE 29-3
STROKE PLAY

If the partners play a stroke or strokes in incorrect order, such stroke or strokes shall be cancelled and *the side shall incur a penalty of two strokes.* The side shall correct the error by playing a ball in correct order as nearly as possible at the spot from which it first played in incorrect order (see Rule 20-5). If the side plays a stroke from the next **teeing ground** without first correcting the error or, in the case of the last hole of the round, leaves the **putting green** without declaring its intention to correct the error, *the side shall be disqualified.*

30 THREE-BALL, BEST-BALL AND FOUR-BALL MATCH PLAY

DEFINITIONS

Three-Ball: A match play competition in which three play against one another, each playing his own ball. Each player is playing two distinct matches.
Best-Ball: A match in which one plays against the better ball of two or the best ball of three players.

BREACH OF RULE BY ONE PARTNER IN MATCH PLAY

I'll just remove this twig.

I'm afraid you're disqualified from the hole for removing a loose impediment from the bunker. Fortunately, although I'm in the same bunker I'm not penalised because your breach of a rule did not assist my play.

Four-Ball: A match in which two play their better ball against the better ball of two other players.

RULE 30-1
RULES OF GOLF APPLY
The Rules of Golf, so far as they are not at variance with the following special Rules, shall apply to three-ball, best-ball and four-ball matches.

RULE 30-2
THREE-BALL MATCH PLAY

a *Ball at Rest Moved by an Opponent*

Except as otherwise provided in the Rules, if the player's ball is touched or moved by an opponent, his **caddie** or **equipment** other than during search, Rule 18-3b applies. *That opponent shall incur a penalty stroke in his match with the player,* but not in his match with the other opponent.

b *Ball Deflected or Stopped by an Opponent Accidentally*

If a player's ball is accidentally deflected or stopped by an opponent, his caddie or equipment, no penalty shall be incurred. In his match with that opponent the player may play the ball as it lies or, before another stroke is played by either side, he may cancel the stroke and play a ball without penalty as nearly as possible at the spot from which the original ball was last played (see Rule 20-5). In his match with the other opponent, the ball shall be played as it lies.
Exception: Ball striking person attending flagstick — see Rule 17-3b.
(Ball purposely deflected or stopped by an opponent — see Rule 1-2.)

89

THREE BALL MATCH PLAY

A John, my ball has struck your trolley.
What do I do now?
B In your match with me you may either play the
ball as it lies or cancel that stroke and replay it.
In your match with Jim you must play your
original ball as it lies.
A That means I'm going to have two balls in
play at the same time.
B That's right. Rule 30-2b.

FOUR BALL: ONE PLAYER MAY REPRESENT SIDE

Your partner's late. Are you disqualified, or just your partner?

Fortunately, neither of us. Because this is a four-ball match I am entitled to represent the side. Let's start. My partner is allowed to join us later, at the conclusion of a hole.

RULE 30-3
BEST-BALL AND FOUR-BALL MATCH PLAY

a *Representation of Side*

A side may be represented by one partner for all or any part of a match; all partners need not be present. An absent partner may join a match between holes, but not during play of a hole.

b *Maximum of 14 Clubs*

The side shall be penalised for a breach of Rule 4-4 by any partner.

c *Order of Play*

Balls belonging to the same side may be played in the order the side considers best.

d *Wrong Ball*

If a player plays a stroke with a **wrong ball** except in a **hazard**, *he shall be disqualified for that hole,* but his partner incurs no penalty even if the wrong ball belongs to him. If the wrong ball belongs to another player, its owner shall place a ball on the spot from which the wrong ball was first played.

e *Disqualification of Side*

(i)   *A side shall be disqualified* for a breach of any of the following by any partner:

Rule 1-3	Agreement to Waive Rules.
Rule 4-1,-2 or -3	Clubs.
Rule 5-1, or -2	The Ball.
Rule 6-2a	Handicap (playing off higher handicap).
Rule 6-4	Caddie.
Rule 6-7	Undue Delay; Slow Play (repeated offence).
Rule 14-3	Artificial Devices and Unusual Equipment.

(ii)   *A side shall be disqualified* for a breach of any of the following by

all partners:
Rule 6-3   Time of Starting and Groups.
Rule 6-8   Discontinuance of Play.

f *Effects of Other Penalties*

If a player's breach of a Rule assists his partner's play or adversely affects an opponent's play, *the partner incurs the applicable penalty in addition to any penalty incurred by the player.*

In all other cases where a player incurs a penalty for breach of a Rule, the penalty shall not apply to his partner. Where the penalty is stated to be loss of hole, the effect shall be to disqualify the player for that hole.

g *Another Form of Match Played Concurrently*

In a best-ball or four-ball match when another form of match is played concurrently, the above special Rules shall apply.

FOUR-BALL STROKE PLAY

In four-ball stroke play two competitors play as partners, each playing his own ball. The lower score of the partners is the score for the hole. If one partner fails to complete the play of a hole, there is no penalty.

RULE 31-1
RULES OF GOLF APPLY
The Rules of Golf, so far as they are not at variance with the following special Rules, shall apply to four-ball stroke play.

RULE 31-2
REPRESENTATION OF SIDE
A side may be represented by either partner for all or any part of a **stipulated round**; both partners need not be present. An absent competitor may join his partner between holes, but not during play of a hole.

RULE 31-3
MAXIMUM OF FOURTEEN CLUBS
The side shall be penalised for a breach of Rule 4-4 by either partner.

RULE 31-4
SCORING
The marker is required to record for each hole only the gross score of whichever partner's score is to count. The gross scores to count must be individually identifiable; otherwise *the side shall be disqualified.* Only one of the partners need be responsible for complying with Rule 6-6b.
(Wrong score — see Rule 31-7a.)

RULE 31-5
ORDER OF PLAY
Balls belonging to the same side may be played in the order the side considers best.

FOUR BALL STROKE PLAY

Date _3RD APRIL 1996_

Competition _SPRING OPEN FOUR-BALL_

PLAYER A _J. SUTHERLAND_   Handicap _16_   Strokes _12_

PLAYER B _W. B. TAYLOR_   Handicap _12_   Strokes _9_

Hole	Length Yards	Par	Stroke Index	Gross Score A	Gross Score B	Net Score A	Net Score B	Won X Lost – Half O	Mar. Score	Hole	Length Yards	Par	Stroke Index	Gross Score A	Gross Score B	Net Score A	Net Score B	Won X Lost – Half O	Mar. Score
1	437	4	4		4		3			10	425	4	3	5		4			
2	320	4	14		4		4			11	141	3	17	3		3			
3	162	3	18		4		4			12	476	5	9	6		5			
4	504	5	7	6		5				13	211	3	11		4		4		
5	181	3	16	4		4				14	437	4	5		5		4		
6	443	4	2		5		4			15	460	4	1		5		4		
7	390	4	8		5		4			16	176	3	15	4		4			
8	346	4	12	5		4				17	340	4	13	4		4			
9	340	4	10	4		3				18	435	4	6	6		5			
Out	3123	35				35				In	3101	34				37			
										Out	3123	35				35			
										T'tl	6224	69				72			

Player's Signature _J. Sutherland_

Marker's Signature _R. J. Parker_

Handicap

Net Score

PARTNER'S SCORES TO BE INDIVIDUALLY IDENTIFIED

1 The lower score of the partners is the score for the hole(Rule 31)

2 Only one of the partners need be responsible for complying with Rule 6-6b i.e. recording scores, checking scores, countersigning and returning the card (Rule 31-4).

3 The competitor is solely responsible for the correctness of the gross score recorded. Although there is no objection to the competitor (or his marker) entering the net score, it is the Committee's responsibility to record the better ball score for each hole, to add up the scores and to apply the handicaps recorded on the card (Rule 33-5). Thus there is no penalty for an error by the competitor (or his marker) for recording an incorrect net score.

4 Scores of the two partners must be kept in separate columns otherwise it is impossible for the Committee to apply the correct handicap. If the scores of both partners, having different handicaps, are recorded in the same column, the Committee has no alternative but to disqualify both partners (Rules 31-7 and 6-6 apply).

5 The Committee is responsible for laying down the conditions under which a competition is to be played (Rule 33-1), including the method of handicapping. In the above illustration the Committee laid down that 3/4 handicaps would apply.

RULE 31-6
WRONG BALL

If a competitor plays a stroke or strokes with a **wrong ball** except in a **hazard**, *he shall add two penalty strokes to his score for the hole* and shall then play the correct ball. His partner incurs no penalty even if the wrong ball belongs to him.

If the wrong ball belongs to another competitor, its owner shall place a ball on the spot from which the wrong ball was first played.

RULE 31-7
DISQUALIFICATION PENALTIES

a *Breach by One Partner*

A side shall be disqualified from the competition for a breach of any of the following by either partner:

Rule 1-3	Agreement to Waive Rules.
Rule 3-4	Refusal to Comply with Rule.
Rule 4-1,-2 or -3	Clubs.
Rule 5-1 or -2	The Ball.
Rule 6-2b	Handicap (playing off higher handicap; failure to record handicap).
Rule 6-4	Caddie.
Rule 6-6b	Signing and Returning Card.
Rule 6-6d	Wrong Score for Hole, i.e. when the recorded score of the partner whose score is to count is lower than actually taken. If the recorded score of the partner whose score is to count is higher than actually taken, it must stand as returned.
Rule 6-7	Undue Delay; Slow Play (repeated offence).
Rule 7-1	Practice Before or Between Rounds.
Rule 14-3	Artificial Devices and Unusual Equipment.
Rule 31-4	Gross Scores to count Not Individually Identifiable.

b *Breach by Both Partners*

A side shall be disqualified:
(i)   for a breach by both partners of Rule 6-3 (Time of Starting and Groups) or Rule 6-8 (Discontinuance of Play), or
(ii) if, at the same hole, each partner is in breach of a Rule the penalty for which is disqualification from the competition or for a hole.

c *For the Hole Only*

In all other cases where a breach of a Rule would entail disqualification, *the competitor shall be disqualified only for the hole at which the breach occurred.*

RULE 31-8
EFFECT OF OTHER PENALTIES

If a competitor's breach of a Rule assists his partner's play, *the partner incurs the applicable penalty in addition to any penalty incurred by the competitor.*

In all other cases where a competitor incurs a penalty for breach of a Rule, the penalty shall not apply to his partner.

BOGEY, PAR AND STABLEFORD COMPETITIONS

RULE 32-1
CONDITIONS

Bogey, par and Stableford competitions are forms of stroke competition in which play is against a fixed score at each hole. The Rules for stroke play, so far as they are not at variance with the following special Rules, apply.

a *Bogey and Par Competitions*

The reckoning for bogey and par competitions is made as in match play. Any hole for which a competitor makes no return shall be regarded as a loss. The winner is the competitor who is most successful in the aggregate of holes.

The marker is responsible for marking only the gross number of strokes for each hole where the competitor makes a net score equal to or less than the fixed score.

Note: Maximum of 14 Clubs – Penalties as in match play – see Rule 4-4.

b *Stableford Competitions*

The reckoning in Stableford competitions is made by points awarded in relation to a fixed score at each hole as follows:

Hole Played in	Points
More than one over fixed score or no score returned	0
One over fixed score	1
Fixed Score	2
One under fixed score	3
Two under fixed score	4
Three under fixed score	5
Four under fixed score	6

The winner is the competitor who scores the highest number of points.

The marker shall be responsible for marking only the gross number of strokes at each hole where the competitor's net score earns one or more points.

Note: Maximum of 14 Clubs (Rule 4-4) – Penalties applied as follows: From total points scored for the round, deduction of two points for each hole at which any breach occurred; maximum deduction per round: four points.

RULE 32-2
DISQUALIFICATION PENALTIES

a *From the Competition*

A competitor shall be disqualified from the competition for a breach of any of the following:

Rule 1-3	Agreement to Waive Rules.
Rule 3-4	Refusal to Comply with Rule.
Rule 4-1, -2 or -3	Clubs.
Rule 5-1 or -2	The Ball.
Rule 6-2b	Handicap (playing off higher handicap; failure to record handicap).

Rule 6-3	Time of Starting and Groups.
Rule 6-4	Caddie.
Rule 6-6b	Signing and Returning Card.
Rule 6-6d	Wrong Score for Hole, except that no penalty shall be incurred when a breach of this Rule does not affect the result of the hole.
Rule 6-7	Undue Delay; Slow Play (repeated offence).
Rule 6-8	Discontinuance of Play.
Rule 7-1	Practice Before or Between Rounds.
Rule 14-3	Artificial Devices and Unusual Equipment.

b *For a Hole*

In all other cases where a breach of a Rule would entail disqualification, *the competitor shall be disqualified only for the hole at which the breach occurred.*

THE COMMITTEE

RULE 33-1
CONDITIONS; WAIVING RULE

The Committee shall lay down the conditions under which a competition is to be played.

The Committee has no power to waive a Rule of Golf. Certain special rules governing stroke play are so substantially different from those governing match play that combining the two forms of play is not practicable and is not permitted. The results of matches played and the scores returned in these circumstances shall not be accepted.

In stroke play the Committee may limit a referee's duties.

RULE 33-2
THE COURSE

a *Defining Bounds and Margins*

The Committee shall define accurately:

(i)   the **course** and **out of bounds**,

(ii)   the margins of **water hazards** and **lateral water hazards**,

(iii)   **ground under repair**, and

(iv)   **obstructions** and integral parts of the course.

b *New Holes*

New holes should be made on the day on which a stroke competition begins and at such other times as the Committee considers necessary, provided all competitors in a single round play with each hole cut in the same position.

Exception: When it is impossible for a damaged hole to be repaired so that it conforms with the Definition, the Committee may make a new hole in a nearby similar position.

Note: Where a single round is to be played on more than one day, the Committee may provide in the conditions of a competition that the holes and teeing grounds may be differently situated on each day of the competition, provided that, on any one day, all competitors play with each hole and each teeing ground in the same position.

COURSE UNPLAYABLE

If the Committee considers the course to be unplayable, it must also decide whether play should be temporarily suspended and then resumed at a later time, or whether play should be declared null and void and all scores for the round cancelled.

c *Practice Ground*

Where there is no practice ground available outside the area of a competition **course**, the Committee should lay down the area on which players may practise on any day of a competition, if it is practicable to do so. On any day of a stroke competition, the Committee should not normally permit practice on or to a **putting green** or from a **hazard** of the competition course.

d *Course Unplayable*

If the Committee or its authorised representative considers that for any reason the course is not in a playable condition, or that there are circumstances which render the proper playing of the game impossible, it may, in match play or stroke play, order a temporary suspension of play or, in stroke play, declare play null and void and cancel all scores for the round in question. When play has been temporarily suspended, it shall be resumed from where it was discontinued, even though resumption occurs on a subsequent day. When a round is cancelled all penalties incurred in that round are cancelled. (Procedure in discontinuing play — see Rule 6-8.)

RULE 33-3
TIMES OF STARTING AND GROUPS
The Committee shall lay down the times of starting and, in stroke play, arrange the groups in which competitors shall play.

When a match play competition is played over an extended period, the Committee shall lay down the limit of time within which each round shall be completed. When players are allowed to arrange the date of their match within these limits, the Committee should announce that the match must be played at a stated time on the last day of the period unless the players agree to a prior date.

RULE 33-4
HANDICAP STROKE TABLE
The Committee shall publish a table indicating the order of holes at which handicap strokes are to be given or received

RULE 33-5
SCORE CARD

In stroke play, the Committee shall issue for each competitor a score card containing the date and the competitor's name or, in foursome or four-ball stroke play, the competitors' names.

In stroke play, the Committee is responsible for the addition of scores and application of the handicap recorded on the card.

In four-ball stroke play, the Committee is responsible for recording the better-ball score for each hole and in the process applying the handicaps recorded on the card, and adding the better-ball scores.

In bogey, par and Stableford competitions, the Committee is responsible for applying the handicap recorded on the card and determining the result of each hole and the overall result or points total.

RULE 33-6
DECISION OF TIES

The Committee shall announce the manner, day and time for the decision of a halved match or of a tie, whether played on level terms or under handicap.

A halved match shall not be decided by stroke play. A tie in stroke play shall not be decided by a match.

RULE 33-7
DISQUALIFICATION PENALTY; COMMITTEE DISCRETION

A penalty of disqualification may in exceptional individual cases be waived, modified or imposed if the Committee considers such action warranted.

Any penalty less than disqualification shall not be waived or modified.

RULE 33-8
LOCAL RULES

a *Policy*

The Committee may make and publish Local Rules for abnormal conditions if they are consistent with the policy of the Governing Authority for the country concerned as set forth in Appendix I to these Rules.

b *Waiving Penalty*

A penalty imposed by a Rule of Golf shall not be waived by a Local Rule.

34

DISPUTES AND DECISIONS

RULE 34-1
CLAIMS AND PENALTIES

a *Match Play*

In match play if a claim is lodged with the Committee under Rule 2-5, a decision should be given as soon as possible so that the state of the match may, if necessary, be adjusted.

If a claim is not made within the time limit provided by Rule 2-5, it shall not be considered unless it is based on facts previously unknown to the player making the claim and the player making the claim had been given wrong information (Rules 6-2a and 9) by an opponent. In any case, no later claim shall be considered after the result of the match has been officially announced, unless the Committee is satisfied that the opponent knew he was giving wrong information.

There is no time limit on applying the disqualification penalty for a breach of Rule 1-3.

b *Stroke Play*

Except as provided below, in stroke play, no penalty shall be rescinded, modified or imposed after the competition has closed. A competition is deemed to have closed when the result has been officially announced or, in stroke play qualifying followed by match play, when the player has teed off in his first match.

Exceptions: A penalty of disqualification shall be imposed after the competition has closed if a competitor:

(i)   was in breach of Rule 1-3 (Agreement to Waive Rules); or

(ii)   returned a score card on which he had recorded a handicap which, before the competition closed, he knew was higher than that to which he was entitled, and this affected the number of strokes received (Rule 6-2b); or

(iii)   returned a score for any hole lower than actually taken (Rule 6-6d) for any reason other than failure to include a penalty which, before the competition closed, he did not know he had incurred; or

(iv)   knew, before the competition closed, that he had been in breach of any other Rule for which the prescribed penalty is disqualification.

RULE 34-2
REFEREE'S DECISION

If a referee has been appointed by the Committee, his decision shall be final.

RULE 34-3
COMMITTEE'S DECISION

In the absence of a referee, any dispute or doubtful point on the Rules shall be referred to the Committee, whose decision shall be final.

If the Committee cannot come to a decision, it shall refer the dispute or doubtful point to the Rules of Golf Committee of the Royal and Ancient Golf Club of St. Andrews, whose decision shall be final.

If the dispute or doubtful point has not been referred to the Rules of Golf Committee, the player or players have the right to refer an agreed statement through the Secretary of the Club to the Rules of Golf Committee for an opinion as to the correctness of the decision given. The reply will be sent to the Secretary of the Club or Clubs concerned.

If play is conducted other than in accordance with the Rules of Golf, the Rules of Golf Committee will not give a decision on any question.

APPENDIX I

LOCAL RULES (RULE 33-8) AND CONDITIONS OF THE COMPETITION (RULE 33-1)

PART A **LOCAL RULES**

Rule 33-8 provides; "The Committee may make and publish Local Rules for abnormal conditions if they are consistent with the policy of the Governing Authority for the country concerned as set forth in Appendix I to these Rules. A penalty imposed by a Rule of Golf shall not be waived by a Local Rule.

Such abnormal conditions may include those listed below. Otherwise, detailed information regarding acceptable and prohibited Local Rules is provided in "Decisions on the Rules of Golf" under Rule 33-8.

If local conditions interfere with the proper playing of the game and it is considered necessary to modify a Rule of Golf, the approval of the Governing Authority must be obtained.

1 **OBSTRUCTIONS**

a *General*

Clarifying the status of objects which may be obstructions (Rule 24).

Declaring any construction to be an integral part of the course and, accordingly, not an obstruction, e.g. built-up sides of teeing grounds, putting greens and bunkers (Rules 24 and 33-2a).

b *Stones in Bunkers*

Allowing the removal of stones in bunkers by declaring them to be "movable obstructions" (Rule 24).

c *Roads and Paths*

(i) Declaring artificial surfaces and sides of roads and paths to be integral parts of the course, or

(ii) Providing relief of the type afforded under Rule 24-2b from roads and paths not having artificial surfaces and sides if they could unfairly affect play

d *Fixed Sprinkler Heads*

Providing relief from intervention by fixed sprinkler heads within two club-lengths of the putting green when the ball lies within two club-lengths of the sprinkler head

e *Protection of Young Trees*

Providing relief for the protection of young trees.

f *Temporary Obstructions*

Specimen Local Rules for temporary obstructions (eg grandstands, television cables and equipment, etc) for application in Tournament Play are available from the Royal and Ancient Golf Club of St. Andrews.

2 **AREAS OF THE COURSE REQUIRING PRESERVATION**

Assisting preservation of the course by defining areas, including turf nurseries, young plantations and other parts of the course under cultivation, as "ground under repair" from which play is prohibited.

3 UNUSUAL DAMAGE TO THE COURSE OR ACCUMULATION OF LEAVES OR THE LIKE

Declaring such areas to be "ground under repair" (Rule 25). The Committee may, by Local Rule, deny relief from interference with a player's stance by such areas – see Note to Rule 25–1a.*Note:* For relief from aeration holes see Specimen Local Rule 8 in Part B of this Appendix.

4 EXTREME WETNESS, MUD, POOR CONDITIONS AND PROTECTION OF COURSE

a *Lifting an Embedded Ball, cleaning*

Where the ground is unusually soft, the Committee may, by temporary Local Rule, allow the lifting of a ball which is embedded in its own pitch-mark in the ground in an area "through the green" which is not "closely mown" (Rule 25-2) if it is satisfied that the proper playing of the game would otherwise be prevented. The Local Rule shall be for that day only or for a short period, and if practicable shall be confined to specified areas. The Committee shall withdraw the Local Rule as soon as conditions warrant and should not print it on the score card.

In similarly adverse conditions, the Committee may, by temporary Local Rule, permit the cleaning of a ball "through the green".

b *"Preferred Lies" and "Winter Rules"*

Adverse conditions, including the poor condition of the course or the existence of mud, are sometimes so general, particularly during winter months, that the Committee may decide to grant relief by temporary Local Rule either to protect the course or to promote fair and pleasant play. Such Local Rule shall be withdrawn as soon as conditions warrant.

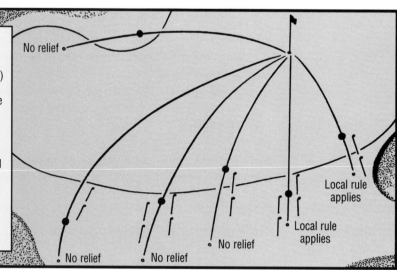

A player is entitled to relief from a fixed sprinkler head (an immovable obstruction) under Rule 24-2. If the specimen Local Rule is introduced, a player is also entitled to relief for intervention to his line of play provided:
(**a**) the fixed sprinkler head is on or within two club-lengths of the putting green; and
(**b**) the ball lies within two club-lengths of the fixed sprinkler head.

5 ENVIRONMENTALLY-SENSITIVE AREAS

When the Committee is required to prohibit play from environmentally-sensitive areas which are on or adjoin the course, it should make a Local Rule clarifying the relief procedure.

An environmentally-sensitive area is an area so declared by an appropriate authority, entry into and/or play from which is prohibited for environmental

ENVIRONMENTALLY-SENSITIVE AREAS

If there is an environmentally-sensitive area on or adjoining a course the Committee should make a Local Rule prohibiting entry into and play from the area and clarifying the relief procedure. In doing so, the Committee should attempt to preserve the character of the hole. As examples:
(**a**) A small area of rare plants – ground under repair;
(**b**) A large area of sand dunes – out of bounds; and
(**c**) A large area of wetlands – water hazard.

reasons. Such an area may be defined as ground under repair, a water hazard, a lateral water hazard or out of bounds at the discretion of the Committee provided that, in the case of an environmentally-sensitive area which has been defined as water hazard or a lateral water hazard, the area is, by Definition, a water hazard.

Note: The Committee may not declare an area to be environmentally-sensitive.

A specimen Local Rule is detailed in " Decisions on the Rules of Golf". Other matters which the Committee could cover by Local Rules include:

6   **WATER HAZARDS**

a *Lateral Water Hazards*   Clarifying the status of sections of water hazards which may be lateral water hazards (Rule 26).

b *Provisional Ball*   Permitting play of a provisional ball for a ball which may be in a water hazard of such character that it would be impracticable to determine whether the ball is in the hazard or to do so would unduly delay play. In such a case, if a provisional ball is played and the original ball is in a water hazard, the player may play the original ball as it lies or continue the provisional ball in play, but he may not proceed under Rule 26-1.

7   **DEFINING BOUNDS AND MARGINS**

Specifying means used to define out of bounds, hazards, water hazards, lateral water hazards and ground under repair.

8   **DROPPING ZONES**

Establishing special areas in which balls may or shall be dropped when it is not feasible or practicable to proceed exactly in conformity with Rule 24-2b (Immovable Obstruction), Rule 25-lb or Rule 25-1c (Ground Under Repair), Rule 25-3 (Wrong Putting Green), Rule 26-1 (Water Hazards and Lateral Water Hazards) or Rule 28 (Ball Unplayable).

9   **PRIORITY ON THE COURSE**

The Committee may make regulations governing Priority on the Course (see Etiquette).

PART B   **SPECIMEN LOCAL RULES**

Within the policy set out in Part A of this Appendix, the Committee may adopt a Specimen Local Rule by referring, on a score card or notice board, to the examples given below. However, Specimen Local Rules 5, 6 or 7 should not be printed or referred to on a score card as they are all of limited duration.

1   **FIXED SPRINKLER HEADS**

All fixed sprinkler heads are immovable obstructions and relief from interference by them may be obtained under Rule 24-2. In addition, if such an obstruction on or within two club-lengths of the putting green of the hole being played intervenes on the line of play between the ball and the hole, the player may obtain relief, without penalty, as follows:

If the ball lies off the putting green but not in a hazard and is within two club-lengths of the intervening obstruction, it may be lifted, cleaned and dropped at the nearest point to where the ball lay which (a) is not nearer the hole, (b) avoids such intervention and (c) is not in a hazard or on a putting green.

PENALTY FOR BREACH OF LOCAL RULE: *Match play – Loss of hole; Stroke play – Two strokes.*

2 | **STONES IN BUNKERS**

Stones in bunkers are movable obstructions (Rule 24-1 applies).

3 | **PROTECTION OF YOUNG TREES**

Protection of young trees identified by_____ . If such a tree interferes with a player's stance or the area of his intended swing, the ball must be lifted, without penalty, and dropped in accordance with the procedure prescribed in Rule 24-2b(i) (Immovable Obstruction).
The ball may be cleaned when so lifted.

PENALTY FOR BREACH OF LOCAL RULE: *Match play – Loss of hole; Stroke play – Two strokes.*

4 | **GROUND UNDER REPAIR: PLAY PROHIBITED**

If a player's ball lies in an area of "ground under repair" from which play is prohibited, or if such an area of "ground under repair" interferes with the player's stance or the area of his intended swing the player must take relief under Rule 25-1.

PENALTY FOR BREACH OF LOCAL RULE: *Match play – Loss of hole; Stroke play – Two strokes.*

5 | **LIFTING AN EMBEDDED BALL**

[*Specify the area if practicable*]. . . through the green, a ball embedded in its own pitch-mark in ground other than sand may be lifted, cleaned and dropped, without penalty, as near as possible to the spot where it lay but not nearer the hole.

PENALTY FOR BREACH OF LOCAL RULE: *Match play – Loss of hole; Stroke play – Two strokes.*

6 | **CLEANING BALL**

[*Specify the area if practicable*]. . . through the green a ball may be lifted, cleaned and replaced without penalty.

Note: The position of the ball shall be marked before it is lifted under this Local Rule – see Rule 20-1.

7 | **"PREFERRED LIES" AND "WINTER RULES"**

A ball lying on any "closely mown area" through the green may, without penalty, be moved or may be lifted, cleaned and placed within six inches of where it originally lay, but not nearer the hole. After the ball has been so moved or placed, it is in play.

PENALTY FOR BREACH OF LOCAL RULE: *Match play – Loss of hole; Stroke play – Two strokes.*

8 | **AERATION HOLES**

If a ball comes to rest in an aeration hole, the player may, without penalty, lift the ball and clean it. Through the green, the player shall drop the ball as near as possible to where it lay, but not nearer the hole. On the putting green, the player shall place the ball at the nearest spot not nearer the hole which avoids such situation.

PENALTY FOR BREACH OF LOCAL RULE: *Match play – Loss of hole; Stroke play – Two strokes.*

PART C | **CONDITIONS OF THE COMPETITION**

Rule 33-1 provides, "The Committee shall lay down the conditions under which a competition is to be played". Such conditions should include many matters such as method of entry, eligibility, number of rounds to be played, settling ties, etc. which it is not appropriate to deal with in the Rules of Golf or this Appendix. Detailed information regarding such conditions is provided in " Decisions on the Rules of Golf" under Rule 33-1.

However, there are seven matters which might be covered in the Conditions of the Competition to which the Committee's attention is specifically drawn by way of a Note to the appropriate Rule. These are:

1 | **SPECIFICATION OF THE BALL (NOTE TO RULE 5-1)**

a. List of Conforming Golf Balls

Arising from the regulations for ball-testing under Rule 5-1, a List of Conforming Golf Balls will be issued from time to time.

It is recommended that the List should be applied to all National and County (or equivalent) Championships and to all top class events when restricted to low handicap players. In order to apply the List to a particular competition the Committee must lay this down in the Conditions of the Competition. This should be referred to in the Entry Form, and also a notice should be displayed on the Club notice board and at the 1st Tee along the following lines:

[*Name of Event*]

[*Date and Club*]

"The Ball (Note to Rule 5-1)

The ball the player uses shall be named on the current List of Conforming Golf Balls issued by the Royal and Ancient Golf Club of St. Andrews."

A penalty statement will be required and must be either:

(a) "**PENALTY FOR BREACH OF CONDITION**: *Disqualification.*"

or

(b) "**PENALTY FOR BREACH OF CONDITION**:

Match play – Loss of each hole at which a breach occurred.

Stroke play – Two strokes for each hole at which a breach occurred".

If option (b) is adopted this only applies to use of a ball which, whilst not on the List of Conforming Golf Balls, does conform to the requirements specified in Rule 5 and Appendix III. The penalty for use of a ball which does not so conform is disqualification.

b. One Ball Condition

If it is desired to prohibit changing brands and types of golf balls during a stipulated round, the following condition is recommended:

"Limitation on Balls used During Round: (Note to Rule 5-1)

(i) "One Ball" Condition

During a stipulated round, the ball the player uses must be of the same brand and type as detailed by a single entry on the current List of Conforming Golf Balls.

PENALTY FOR BREACH OF CONDITION:

Match Play – At the conclusion of the hole at which the breach is discovered, the state of the match shall be adjusted by deducting one hole for each hole at which a breach occurred; maximum deduction per round: Two holes.

Stroke Play – Two strokes for each hole at which any breach occurred; maximum penalty per round; Four strokes.

(ii) Procedure when breach discovered

When a player discovers that he has used a ball in breach of this condition, he shall abandon that ball before playing from the next teeing ground and complete the round using a proper ball; otherwise, the player shall be disqualified. If discovery is made during play of a hole and the player elects to substitute a proper ball before completing that hole, the player shall place a proper ball on the spot where the ball used in breach of the condition lay.'

Note: In Club events it is recommended that no such conditions be applied.

2   TIME OF STARTING (NOTE TO RULE 6-3a)

If the Committee wishes to act in accordance with the Note, the following wording is recommended:

"If the player arrives at his starting point, ready to play, within five minutes after his starting time, in the absence of circumstances which warrant waiving the penalty of disqualification as provided in Rule 33-7, the penalty for failure to start on time is loss of the first hole to be played in match play or two strokes in stroke play. Penalty for lateness beyond five minutes is disqualification".

3 | **PACE OF PLAY**

The Committee may lay down pace of play guidelines, to help prevent slow play, in accordance with Note 2 to Rule 6-7.

4 | **SUSPENSION OF PLAY DUE TO A DANGEROUS SITUATION (NOTE TO RULE 6-8b)**

If the Committee wishes to act in accordance with the Note, the following wording is recommended:

"When play is suspended by the Committee for a dangerous situation (eg lightning, tornado, etc) if the players in a match or group are between the play of two holes, they shall not resume play until the Committee has ordered a resumption of play. If they are in the process of playing a hole, they shall discontinue play immediately and shall not thereafter resume play until the Committee has ordered a resumption of play.

The signal for suspending play due to a dangerous situation will be............
PENALTY FOR BREACH OF CONDITION: Disqualification

5 | **PRACTICE**

The Committee may make regulations governing practice in accordance with the Note to Rule 7-1, Exception (c) to Rule 7-2, Note 2 to Rule 7 and Rule 33-2c.

6 | **ADVICE IN TEAM COMPETITIONS**

If the Committee wishes to act in accordance with the Note, the following wording is recommended:

"In accordance with the Note to Rule 8 of the Rules of Golf each team may appoint one person (in addition to the persons from whom advice may be asked under that Rule) who may give advice to members of that team. Such person [*if it is desired to insert any restriction on who may be nominated insert such restriction here*] shall be identified to the Committee before giving advice."

7 | **NEW HOLES**

The Committee may provide, in accordance with the Note to Rule 33-2b, that the holes and teeing grounds for a single round competition, being held on more than one day, may be differently situated on each day.

APPENDICES II & III

Any design in a club or ball which is not covered by Rules 4 and 5 and Appendices II and III, or which might significantly change the nature of the game, will be ruled on by the Royal and Ancient Golf Club of St. Andrews and the United States Golf Association.

APPENDIX II

DESIGN OF CLUBS

Clubs must not be substantially different from the traditional and customary form and make.

Rule 4-1 prescribes general regulations for their design. The following paragraphs, which provide some specifications and clarify how Rule 4-1 is interpreted, should be read in conjunction with that Rule.

Where a club, or part of a club, is required to have some specific property, this means that it must be designed and manufactured with the intention of having that property. The finished club or part must have that property within manufacturing tolerances appropriate to the material used.

RULE 4-1a
GENERAL

Adjustability-Exception for Putters: Clubs other than putters shall not be designed to be adjustable except for weight. Some other forms of adjustability are permitted in the design of a putter, provided that:

(i)   the adjustment cannot be readily made;

(ii)   all adjustable parts are firmly fixed and there is no reasonable likelihood of them working loose during a round; and

(iii)   all configurations of adjustment conform with the Rules.

The disqualification penalty for purposely changing the playing characteristics of a club during a stipulated round (Rule 4-2) applies to all clubs including a putter.

Note: It is recommended that all putters with adjustable parts be submitted to the Royal and Ancient Golf Club of St. Andrews for a ruling.

RULE 4-1b
SHAFT

Straightness: The shaft shall be straight from the top of the grip to a point not more than 5 inches (127mm) above the sole, measured from the point where the shaft ceases to be straight along the axis of the bent part of the shaft and the neck and/or socket (see Fig. I).

Length: The overall length of the club shall be at least 18 inches (457mm) measured from the top of the grip along the axis of the shaft or a straight line extension of it to the sole of the club.

Alignment: When the club is in its normal address position the shaft shall be so aligned that:
(i)   the projection of the straight part of the shaft on to the vertical plane through the toe and heel shall diverge from the vertical by a least 10 degrees. (See Fig. II)
(ii)   the projection of the straight part of the shaft on to the vertical plane along the intended line of play shall not diverge from the vertical by more than 20 degrees. (See Fig. III)
Except for putters, all of the heel portion of the club shall lie within 0.625 inches (16mm) of the plane containing the axis of the straight part of the shaft and the intended (horizontal) line of play. (See Fig. IV)

Bending and Twisting Properties: At any point along its length, the shaft shall:
(i)   bend in such a way that the deflection is the same regardless of how the shaft is rotated about its longitudinal axis, and
(ii)   twist the same amount in both directions.

Attachment to Clubhead: The shaft shall be attached to the clubhead at the heel either directly or through a neck and/or socket. The length from the top of the neck and/or socket to the sole of the club shall not exceed 5 inches (127mm), measured along the axis of, and following any bend in, the neck and/or socket. (See Fig.V)
Exception for Putters: The shaft or neck or socket of a putter may be fixed at any point in the head.

RULE 4-1c
GRIP (See Fig VI)
(i)   For clubs other than putters the grip must be circular in cross-section, except that a continuous, straight, slightly raised rib may be incorporated along the full length of the grip, and a slightly indented spiral is permitted on a wrapped grip or a replica of one.
(ii)   A putter grip may have a non-circular cross-section, provided the cross-section has no concavity, is symmetrical and remains generally similar throughout the length of the grip.
(iii)   The grip may be tapered but must not have any bulge or waist. Its cross-sectional dimension measured in any direction must not exceed 1.75 inches (45mm).
(iv)   For clubs other than putters the axis of the grip must coincide with the axis of the shaft.
(v)   A putter may have more than one grip, provided each is circular in cross-section and the axis of each coincides with the axis of the shaft.

RULE 4-1d
CLUBHEAD
Dimensions: The dimensions of a clubhead are measured, with the clubhead in its normal address position, on horizontal lines between vertical projections

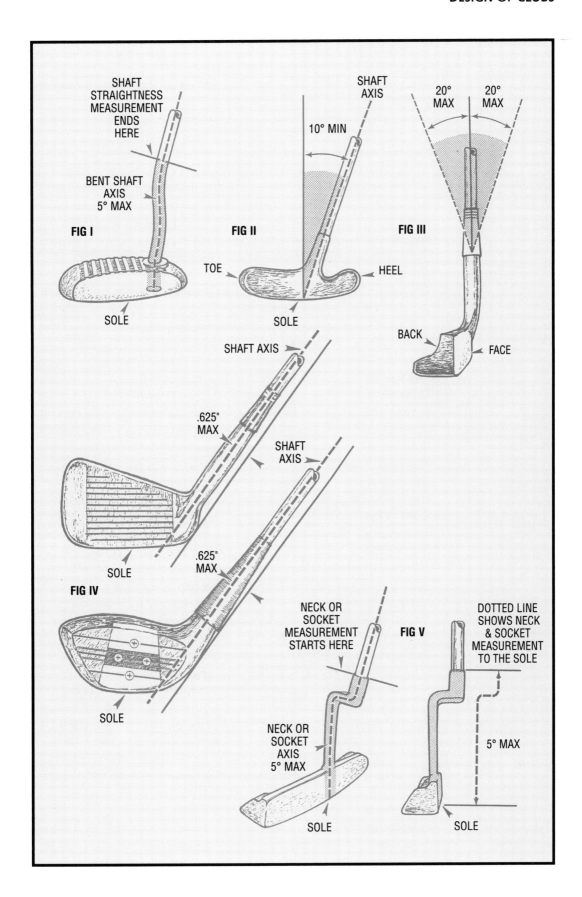

SHAFT
STRAIGHTNESS
MEASUREMENT
ENDS
HERE

BENT SHAFT
AXIS
5° MAX

FIG I

SOLE

SHAFT
AXIS

10° MIN

TOE

HEEL

SOLE

FIG II

20°
MAX

20°
MAX

FIG III

BACK

FACE

SHAFT AXIS

.625"
MAX

SHAFT
AXIS

SOLE

FIG IV

.625"
MAX

SOLE

NECK OR
SOCKET
MEASUREMENT
STARTS HERE

FIG V

NECK OR
SOCKET
AXIS
5° MAX

SOLE

DOTTED LINE
SHOWS NECK
& SOCKET
MEASUREMENT
TO THE SOLE

5° MAX

SOLE

of the outermost points of (i) the heel and the toe and (ii) the face and the back (See Fig VII, dimension A). If the outermost point of the heel is not clearly defined, it is deemed to be 0.625 inches (16mm) above the horizontal plane on which the club is resting in its normal address position (See Fig VII, dimension B).

Plain in Shape: The clubhead shall be generally plain in shape. All parts shall be rigid, structural in nature and functional.

It is not practicable to define plain in shape precisely and comprehensively but features which are deemed to be in breach of this requirement and are therefore not permitted include:

(a)   holes through the head,

(b)   transparent material added for other than decorative or structural purposes,

(c)   appendages to the main body of the head such as knobs, plates, rods or fins, for the purpose of meeting dimensional specifications, for aiming or for any other purpose. Exceptions may be made for putters.

Any furrows in or runners on the sole shall not extend into the face.

RULE 4-1e
CLUB FACE

General: The material and construction of the face shall not have the effect at impact of a spring, or impart significantly more spin to the ball than a standard steel face, or have any other effect which would unduly influence the movement of the ball.

Impact Area Roughness and Material: Except for markings specified in the following paragraphs, the surface roughness within the area where impact is intended (the "impact area") must not exceed that of decorative sandblasting, or of fine milling.

The impact area must be of a single material. Exceptions may be made for wooden clubs. (See Fig. VIII, illustrative impact area)

"Impact Area" Markings: Markings in the impact area must not have sharp edges or raised lips as determined by a finger rest. Grooves or punch marks in the impact area must meet the following specifications:

(i)   **Grooves.** A series of straight grooves with diverging sides and a symmetrical cross-section may be used (See Fig. IX). The width and cross-section must be consistent across the face of the club and along the length of the grooves. Any rounding of groove edges shall be in the form of a radius which does not exceed 0.020 inches (0.5mm). The width of the grooves shall not exceed 0.035 inches (0.9mm), using the 30 degree method of measurement on file with the Royal and Ancient Golf Club of St. Andrews. The distance between edges of adjacent grooves must not be less than three times the width of a groove, and not less than 0.075 inches (1.9mm). The depth of a groove must not exceed 0.020 inches (0.5mm).

(ii)   **Punch Marks.** Punch marks may be used. The area of any such mark

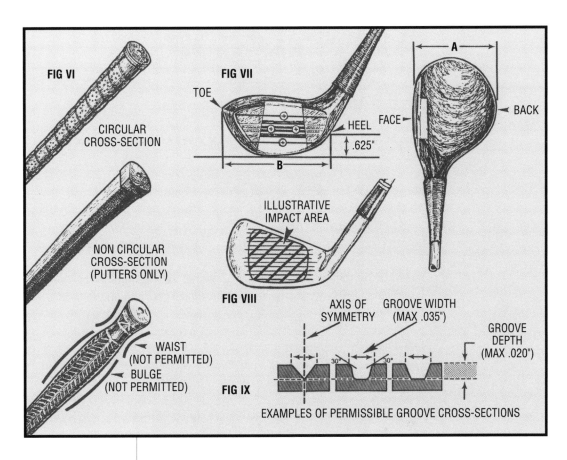

FIG VI

CIRCULAR
CROSS-SECTION

NON CIRCULAR
CROSS-SECTION
(PUTTERS ONLY)

WAIST
(NOT PERMITTED)
BULGE
(NOT PERMITTED)

FIG VII

TOE HEEL FACE .625" BACK A B

ILLUSTRATIVE
IMPACT AREA

FIG VIII

AXIS OF
SYMMETRY

GROOVE WIDTH
(MAX .035")

GROOVE
DEPTH
(MAX .020")

30° 30°

FIG IX

EXAMPLES OF PERMISSIBLE GROOVE CROSS-SECTIONS

must not exceed 0.0044 square inches (2.8 sq.mm). A mark must not be closer to an adjacent mark than 0.168 inches (4.3mm) measured from centre to centre. The depth of a punch mark must not exceed 0.040 inches (1.0mm). If punch marks are used in combination with grooves, a punch mark must not be closer to a groove than 0.168 inches (4.3mm), measured from centre to centre.

Decorative Markings: The centre of the impact area may be indicated by a design within the boundary of a square whose sides are 0.375 inches (9.5mm) in length. Such a design must not unduly influence the movement of the ball. Decorative markings are permitted outside the impact area.

Non-metallic Club Face Markings: The above specifications apply to clubs on which the impact area of the face is of metal or a material of similar hardness. They do not apply to clubs with faces made of other materials and whose loft angle is 24 degrees or less, but markings which could unduly influence the movement of the ball are prohibited. Clubs with this type of face and a loft angle exceeding 24 degrees may have grooves of maximum width 0.040 inches (1.0mm) and maximum depth 1½ times the groove width, but must otherwise conform to the markings specifications above.

Putter Face Markings: The specifications above with regard to club face markings and surface roughness do not apply to putters.

APPENDIX III

THE BALL

Weight: The weight of the ball shall not be greater than 1.620 ounces avoirdupois (45.93gm).

Size: The diameter of the ball shall be not less than 1.680 inches (42.67mm). This specification will be satisfied if, under its own weight, a ball falls through a 1.680 inches diameter ring gauge in fewer than 25 out of 100 randomly selected positions, the test being carried out at a temperature of 23 ± 1°C.

Spherical Symmetry: The ball must not be designed, manufactured or intentionally modified to have properties which differ from those of a spherically symmetrical ball.

Initial Velocity: The velocity of the ball shall not be greater than 250 feet (76.2m) per second when measured on apparatus approved by the Royal and Ancient Golf Club of St. Andrews. A maximum tolerance of 2% will be allowed.
   The temperature of the ball when tested shall be 23 ± 1°C

Overall Distance Standard: A brand of golf ball, when tested on apparatus approved by the Royal and Ancient Golf Club of St. Andrews under the conditions set forth in the Overall Distance Standard for golf balls on file with the Royal and Ancient Golf Club of St. Andrews, shall not cover an average distance in carry and roll exceeding 280 yards (256 metres) plus a tolerance of 6%.
Note: The 6% tolerance will be reduced to a minimum of 4% as test techniques are improved.

HANDICAPS

The Rules of Golf do not legislate for the allocation and adjustment of handicaps or their playing differentials. Such matters are within the jurisdiction and control of the National Union concerned and queries should be directed accordingly.